# REBEL REBEL
## The Billy Morgan Story

With Billy Keane

*Ballpoint Press*

*This book is dedicated to my wife Mary
and my two sons, Brian and Alan*

Published in 2009 by Ballpoint Press
4 Wyndham Park, Bray,
Co Wicklow, Republic of Ireland

ISBN 9 78 0955 02982 0

Typeset by Úna Design

Printed by GraphyCems

© Text copyright Billy Morgan and Billy Keane

Pictures reproduced by kind permission of the 'Irish Examiner',
the 'Irish Independent' and Sportsfile

Cover image by Inpho

Billy Morgan has given his life to Cork football – almost literally.
He suffered a heart attack in 2007, which was kept secret until now,
in the middle of yet another controversy with the Cork County Board.

*Morgan has battled the odds all his life. Sometimes he has found himself suspended or sacked. He acknowledges his temper is his Achilles heel, but it is his honesty both in this book and in his life that has earned him the respect of GAA people.*

In this book, he holds nothing back. He tells it all: from the death of his mother,
to his reaction to a conviction for the assault of a pupil, and then to glory days.
And yet the book is laced with strong Cork humour.

*Morgan just never gives up. Within a few months of his heart attack and the trauma with the Cork County Board, he was back training teams at his beloved Nemo.*

Billy Keane is a Listowel publican who writes a regular sports column for
the 'Irish Independent' and is a frequent contributor to television and radio.

*He has written an acclaimed novel, 'The Last of the Heroes', and co-wrote Moss Keane's best-selling autobiography, 'Rucks, Mauls and Gaelic Footballs'.*

# CONTENTS

# PROLOGUE

## October 2007

Graham Canty, Eoin Sexton and Conor McCarthy called to my office one evening after work.

The three boys were there as representatives of the 2007 Cork football squad. The players decided to fight a campaign, the purpose of which was to force the Cork County Board to revert to the system whereby the manager appointed his own selectors. The players also made it clear they wanted me reinstated as manager.

Just a few weeks previously, I had refused to let my name go forward for the manager's position when the Cork County Board took it upon themselves to appoint the county selectors.

The lads were tense. You could see that they wanted to do what was right. Players just want to play. GAA politics is for the career committee men. I could see the earnestness painted on their faces as they waited for my response. You could see they just wanted to do the right thing, whatever the cost.

I thanked Graham, Eoin and Conor for their support.

It meant so much to me that the players were with me. I was conscious of the fact that players have a short career and that a strike could finish it off altogether, whereas the officials seem to go on forever.

'Lads, ye can't fight a war on two fronts,' I advised. 'Fight the first one first and change the system that was imposed upon ye. Leave my reinstatement out of it, for the moment.'

I swallowed hard when they left. Their visit caught me emotionally on two levels. Firstly, there was the fact they backed me up and secondly I knew only too well what they were up against.

The footballers went on strike and the hurlers joined them in the autumn of 2007. They had no choice.

I didn't have any more to do with the strike after that. Thousands of people marched in favour of the players, but there was still no resolution. It was coming up to Christmas and the Board were adamant they wouldn't change the system.

And then I had a heart attack.

I went out for a run one evening about four weeks after I competed in the New York Marathon and I felt a pain in my chest. I ignored it. Sometimes I suffer from a hiatus hernia and after a few minutes I felt fine. I was running in Nemo a few days later and again I got the pain in the chest. This time I was a little breathless as well.

There was another attack while I was playing golf in Kinsale. This time the pain was even worse. I got the pain while playing the third hole, which was known as heart attack hill. It's a 9-hole course and I got another pain in the chest second time around on the same hole, only this time it was much worse. Just then there was a heavy shower of rain and I took shelter under the trees.

That shower of rain might well have saved my life. If it hadn't rained, I would have kept on going up that hill and God only knows what might have happened. I still didn't think it was a heart attack. I thought it was the hiatus hernia. I made an appointment to see Dr Con Murphy and he called me back fifteen minutes later. He told me he had set up a consultation with Dr Bill Fennell.

'Billy,' said Dr Fennell, 'I think you have angina.'

'I couldn't have. I'm only after running the marathon.'

'I'm telling you, you have angina.'

'But I haven't.'

'I have an appointment for you to do some tests on Friday morning.'

'But I have to go to London on Friday. I have business Friday morning.'

Then he pointed at me and he said with a kind of menace in his voice, 'Forget about your trip to London. You be up here on Friday morning'.

That was on Tuesday. I went back to work and forgot about it.

I got a bad pain on Wednesday and I had to lean up against the wall. And the same thing happened the following day, but I carried on. I still had the attitude that it couldn't be me but I felt absolutely terrible.

I had an angiogram in the Bons Secours hospital on the Friday and Dr Fennell told me I had deteriorated since Tuesday.

'Did anything happen since?'

I told him about the pains and Dr Fennell told me I was after having a heart attack.

He said I had a one hundred per cent blockage in one artery and fifty per cent blockage in another. Dr Fennell called my wife Mary and he told her I would probably need a bypass, but they would try an angioplasty the following day.

I was kept in overnight and I had the angioplasty. You're awake while it's going on. And you're looking up at this screen. I couldn't make anything out of it. Then all of a sudden this Cork nurse started to shout out excitedly.

'Yes, it's working. It's after working. It's after working.'

I didn't have to go for the bypass but the next six months were as tough as I ever spent.

# CHAPTER 1

# *The Pitch*

**I WAS BORN AND REARED IN TONYVILLE TERRACE, OFF HIGH STREET IN CORK CITY.**

My mother Sheila died of a brain tumour just after Christmas in 1951 and left my Dad Tom to look after us. Tony was the eldest, my sister Mary was next, then there was my brother Noel, and I was the youngest, born on February 2, 1945.

I can't remember my mother that much. I was only a month short of my sixth birthday when she died.

I have a vague recollection of the ambulance calling to our house at Tonyville. It was sometime before Christmas and I was only just back from school when they were taking my mother out our front door. I was too young to understand what was really going on.

I'm afraid I have very few memories of my mother. I know that she was looking forward to me making my First Communion, but of course she never lived to see the day.

I can picture my mother and another woman chatting, just up from The Red Gate we used as a goal, near the top of High Street overlooking Cork city. They had a good talk and my mother told her friend I was making my First Communion the following May. That's all I can remember from my mother, even though I am sure she must have said thousands of things to me.

I think she was a tallish, good-looking woman. At least I think she was tall. When you're a small boy, you think all adults are tall.

My father spent a lot of time in the hospital looking after my mother when she had the brain tumour.

My sister Mary and I were sent to my Aunt Mary in Cappataggle, Co Galway while my mother was dying. The two boys stayed with Aunt Delia in nearby Ballydonlon, which meant we weren't really split up and we spent a good bit of time together.

Again I can only barely remember those days. My Aunt Mary and her husband Tony Monaghan were very good to us. Tony was the

1

headmaster in Cappataggle National School and he made sure we kept up with our lessons at the school, which was right next door to the house. My mother died on the 9th of January and we stayed in Galway until my father was able to bring us back to Cork shortly after.

My father went through hell in those terrible times. Years later, my sister Mary gave me a very sad letter Dad wrote to Aunt Mary around the time my mother was in her last days. My father's letter was in his perfect handwriting and it showed how much he cared for us. It was meant as a private letter, and it will remain so. You could see from the letter he was at his wits end trying to sort us out. He never once mentioned himself. The letter was all about my mother and us. It was very emotional when I read it again and I don't really want to go into it any more than that.

My father's family were into sport and he always encouraged us. Dad played junior hurling with Galway. His brothers Mick and Paddy played with the Galway seniors. Uncle Bill played rugby with London Irish and was sub hooker for Ireland on a number of occasions. If it was nowadays, he would have a good few caps, but back then subs weren't allowed to come on.

Uncle Bill became secretary and later president of London Irish. He always sent me a little note congratulating me when I played for Cork. Dad made us aware of the family background in sport and especially hurling without overdoing it, or putting us under pressure.

My first memories of football go way back to around the time when I was about four years of age. My big brother Tony, who was a good player, was six years older than me. Noel, also a fine sportsman, was two years older. I was thrilled at being allowed to play with the boys. I think it was a very important part of my education as a footballer. The two boys never left me out of their games, and I was well used to playing sport from a very early age.

Tony and myself beat Noel and our neighbour Liam Manley in my first big game, which was really no more than a kickabout. I can't be sure when that was, but I got a few goals. I'd definitely say Noel left me in for a few soft ones, just to get me going. And that night my Dad gave me a present of a comic called 'Film Fun'. I loved 'Film Fun'. It had cartoons about Laurel and Hardy, Abbott and Costello and Red Skelton. It meant so much to me. God, it must have been nearly 60 years ago, but I remember it like it was all happening right in front of me.

We played that first game on a rough field in Tonyville Terrace. That was our piece of heaven, our playground, and no matter what time of the day or night you went out, there was always someone to play with. All I had to do was run out our front door and I was on The Pitch in about two seconds.

That's why we called it: The Pitch. I didn't even have to climb a wall. It was nearly our front lawn and if you wanted to, you could view all the action from my upstairs bedroom window.

The field seemed huge back then. I would say it was about three-quarters the size of a soccer pitch, but for us it was Croke Park after an All-Ireland final or Wembley Stadium after the FA Cup final or Lansdowne Road after a rugby international. Our imaginations knew no bounds. We even played cricket there with a hurley and a ball.

It all started on The Pitch.

There were only 18 houses in Tonyville, but kids joined us from the High Street or Higha as we used to call it, Capwell and Windmill Road. The games were intense and you had to fight for every ball. The families were big back then, and there was always a gang of kids out playing. The Pitch was usually threadbare up the centre from all the matches. The goals were usually a couple of stones, or sometimes we used jumpers and coats. At some stage someone made goals and nets, but the nets didn't last too long with all the wear and tear. We played all day during the school holidays and every chance we got during school time.

It wasn't all sport. The girls didn't play football or hurling back then. Their game was pickey, our word for hopscotch. There was skipping too and we often played these games with the girls until we got older. We went to the cinema some Saturdays, when we had the money. The Assembly Rooms Cinema was on The South Mall, right in the city centre. We could be down to The Assembs in ten minutes from Tonyville.

There was the 4d hop, the 6d hop and the shilling hop. Hop was our word for the rows of seats.

We seated ourselves in the middle row, or the sixpenny hops. Half the fun was watching the boys 'going over the back' to the dearer seats. The trick was to wait until the lights were turned out. Then we waited until Georgie, who was the usher, had his back turned. It was only then that you would make your move. We loved the Westerns and Johnny Mack Brown was our favourite cowboy star. I was very shy when I was young. I still am. I didn't say too much, but I loved the comments, I just sat back and took it all in.

In one film Johnny was about to enter a baddies barn and the baddy was hiding behind the door.

The lads couldn't help themselves when they thought Johnny was going to be shot by the baddie. Several small boys stood up and roared, 'Watch out Johnny, he's behind the door!'

When someone was shot, a shout would go up – 'Georgieeeee, remove the body!'

Just when we were about to learn Johnny's fate, the notice we dreaded more than anything came up on the screen: 'To be continued next week'. And we had to find a tanner (sixpence) from somewhere to get back the following Saturday to see if Johnny survived. When the film was over, the posse galloped off up Higha to Dummy's Lane, via Tonyville and The Pitch. We played cowboys there, and in the streets around Tonyville.

There were bushes and corners for hiding out and when you left it to go home, 'you rode out of town down The Pitch'.

We turned every part of our childhood surroundings into a playground.

The house at the end of Tonyville had a long wall and we played handball up against the wall of the Brahalish, which was the name on the house.

'Tip the Can' was one of our favourite games. A tin can was placed on a window sill in Tonyville and if you were 'on', you put your hands up to your eyes and counted 5, 10, 15 . . . up to 100. And then you shouted 'ready or not, I'm coming'. It was like hide and seek, but it was tougher. You had to catch as many as ten or 12 kids. If any kid got back to the can before you, the ones you caught up to that point were set free. And you had to start all over again. There used to be some fierce races for the cans. And if you were 'on' and lost, the frustration of losing would drive you mad. If the boy beat you to the can, he would roar '1. . . 2 . . . 3. Can release'.

\* \* \*

Even though Cork was technically a city, it was really a big town and we knew all our neighbours.

Our next door neighbour was the actor Edward Mulhare who played the part of The Ghost in 'The Ghost and Mrs Muir' and the Chaplain in 'Von Ryan's Express'.

He'd come home every now and then and there would be great excitement in Tonyville.

'The Ed Sullivan Show' came to interview his mother and the TV company handed out cakes and sandwiches. There was a big van at the end of the road, but we had no television back then and we never got to see the interview.

Edward's sister Betty, who would have been much younger than him, came in from next door to take care of us when my mother died. She was very good to us and nearly became like one of the family. Betty did all the cooking and cleaning for a few years, until she got married.

By then we were old enough to almost look after ourselves and my sister Mary picked up where Betty left off. Mary was only a young girl, but she was a very good cook. She was taught by the nuns in home economics classes and she made a roast of beef every Sunday. Mary introduced us to such delights as roast stuffed pork steak, but that was a treat on special occasions. We all gave a hand around the house at the cleaning and the cooking when we were older, even though the boys only ever put on the cabbage or potatoes. Mary was the head cook. And I never once heard her complain about all she had to do.

Tony was only with us at holiday time. When I was seven, he went away to Ballyvourney Secondary School in West Cork on a scholarship. I missed him terribly and counted the days to when he would come home on holiday. I can't say how much I missed him. He was my hero. Tony brought me to matches and to school. I looked up to him. He was on the Scoil Chríost Rí team and I was so proud to be his little brother.

Dad saw it as a great opportunity for Tony to become a teacher as the students in Ballyvourney were groomed for entry into primary teaching. Tony was very bright and he was awarded a scholarship. Of course I didn't understand that at the time and I was very, very lonesome after Tony.

* * *

I started school in Turners Cross Girls Convent. I am told my mother brought me to school every day on a special saddle on the back of her bike – a 'backer' we called it. It seems strange, looking back on it, that I started out school in a convent. That was the way it was when I was a small boy. There were about 40 of us in the 'babies' class and every now and then we played football in a tiny yard. It was pandemonium. Sister Rosario, our teacher, would throw in the ball and you'd go mad trying to get a touch during the game.

From there we were sent to the South Connie or South Convent and we were prepared for our First Communion later that year in Senior Infants.

Our teacher was Sister Benedict and to my dying day I will never forget her. We were afraid of our lives of her. We had to bring a penny every Friday for the black babies, which was a collection for the foreign missions. I forgot it one day and she flaked me for it. I was in her class when my mother died and I have more memories of her than my mother. The kids used to be terrified going into school if we didn't have our lessons done. I would be nearly sick with the thought of facing her. We learned more through being terrified than anything else.

We made our Communion down in the South Church, about ten minutes' walk from Tonyville. After the ceremony we were brought back up into the convent and we were given a cup of some kind of diluted drink and a biscuit. I missed out a bit on the post-Communion financial bonanza when the young lads used to go collecting; all my relations were in Galway so I didn't make as much as the others. There was really only ourselves in Cork.

I went to Scoil Chríost Rí after that. There was slapping if we broke the rules, but nothing major until we hit fifth class and Brother Dermot. He was a terror. The whole school was afraid of him. I met an old school pal, not long after Brother Dermot died just a few years back, and he told me he went down to the funeral.

'You what?' I asked in great surprise.

'Ah Bill,' he replied, 'I was just checking to make sure the f***er was dead.'

I enjoyed running and I represented the school in the City Sports until I was dropped for a new boy who came into the school. Frank Cogan was a flyer, a powerful young fella and he won everything. Little did I think when I saw him come into class on that first day that we would end up winning All-Irelands together, and marrying twin sisters.

Brother Andrew taught me so much about Gaelic football. He was young enough when we knew him first, and he took a fierce interest in us. We nicknamed him Small Dan and he was a Kerryman.

To this day I remember his coaching. He taught us skills such as rising the ball, blocking down a ball, catching it and protecting it with your two hands. Small Dan coached the basics and any fella who played in Críost Rí will tell you just how good a coach he was. He's still to the good and is retired in Cork city.

I trained hard that first year under Small Dan, but I didn't make the school team at Under-13 level.

It was the first time I came into contention for a place. I was about ten. It was back around 1955. There were trials and the squad was whittled down, over about six weeks of hard training.

I desperately wanted to follow in the footsteps of my big brothers. It came down to the last place in the squad. John Daly, who became a country and western singer afterwards, beat me for the spot and I was devastated.

Small Dan called me aside and explained he had to pick John because he was in sixth class and it was his last year in the school, which of course meant it was his last chance to make the school team. Small Dan told me I had another two years at that age level.

'Your turn will come Billy,' he said.

I knew he was right in what he did. I was still hurting, but at least I was given a reason. It was a lesson that stood to me ever after. If you tell players the truth, there's no comeback. I never tell players lies, or make promises I can't keep.

Frank Cogan made the team. He was a year older than me and it was obvious, even at that stage, he was special.

The goalkeeper on that school team was Brendan Nestor who owns a pub down in Kinsale, and he's a great friend of mine. He still slags me over him keeping me off the team, even though I was a forward back then.

I made the team the following year. I was centre-forward and Frank captained us from centre-back. Small Dan was in Canada by then and Brother Vincent was an excellent replacement.

We beat St Joseph's in the final. I was thrilled as Tony and Noel won trophies in the school and it was always my ambition to follow them. After the match, we were brought back into school for milk and cakes. I still have the miniature cup we were given for winning the final. It's in the shape of an egg cup and no bigger than one, but to me it was the Sam Maguire. And for a while, many years later, the Sam sat next to it on our mantlepiece.

The photograph of that winning team is still up on the school wall in Críost Rí. They were a great bunch of lads.

I was playing hurling all along mainly as a half-forward or at midfield among my age group.

My first experience of playing in goal was as a 12-year-old with the Under-14 school hurling team. Brother Vincent must have thought I had a good eye for a ball and so he put me in goal on that team. We won the Cork City schools Under-14 title that year.

That qualified us for the county championship.

We met Cobh in the final. Every year, without fail, we used to beat

Cobh in a challenge game by 20 points. We were so confident of beating them we conceded venue and went down to Cobh on the train to play the final. We were beaten, and we couldn't believe it.

Up to then it was the biggest sporting disappointment of my life. And it nearly still is.

Hurling was my favourite game at that stage. We played mostly hurling and soccer on The Pitch. They were the two big games in the city. Football was the poor relation and hurling was definitely my first love. I came from a hurling background and the Cork hurling team won the three-in-a-row in '52, '53 and '54. They were my heroes, especially Christy Ring.

I was nominated for a football award back around 1991 by the South East Board and Willie John Daly who played on that famous three-in-a row hurling team in the fifties was the recipient of the hurling award. I was absolutely thrilled to be in the same hall as him. We had a great chat that night. I was like a schoolboy, asking him all sorts of questions and hanging on his every word.

\* \* \*

I had soccer heroes too.

I followed Evergreen United ever since they played in the 1953 Cup Final against Cork Athletic. Evergreen were based around Turners Cross, near where we lived, and they changed their name to Cork Celtic in the late fifties.

We used to go to Turners Cross every second Sunday and then when Celtic were away, we would go up to the 'Dyke to cheer for whoever Cork Hibernians were playing. You were either Celtic or Hibs, and we were most definitely Celtic boys.

Celtic had a great team when I was growing up. Donie Leahy and Austin Noonan were my heroes. Paul O'Donovan was a bundle of tricks and a great character. Ray Cowhie and John Coughlan were household names. Mick 'Slap' O'Keeffe and Connie Buckley were fine full-backs. Kevin Blount, who played in goals, used to come to some of the games from Dublin on his motorbike and was accepted as one of our own. Pat O'Mahony, who was in Noel's class in Scoil Chríost Rí, came home from West Ham to play with Celtic. Frankie McCarthy, another Celtic star, was in Tony's class and we knew him well. Gordon O'Flynn came from Hibs. We used to hate him when he played with Hibs, but we loved him when he played with Celtic. Donie Leary, another neighbour, was outside left. Mick Millington, a classy left-half, was a Dub and we took him to our hearts.

In those days, Celtic were truly a neighbourhood team, with the odd Dub or two thrown in.

Little did I think when I was a small boy going to the games at Turners Cross that I would join the club. I was signed as cover for Alex Ludzic by Carl Davenport in the late sixties. I used to train with Ludzic, who was a great 'keeper and taught me a lot back in the days when there were no specialist goalkeeping coaches in the GAA. Alex stayed injury-free and I never got a game.

Thousands used to go to the matches when I was a kid.

There was great banter on the terraces. Paul O'Donovan was being slagged all day by an individual in the crowd.

'You're a langer,' he shouted at Paul.

But there was no jumping the wall like Eric Cantona. Paul relied on his wit.

'You must be a bigger langer than me so?' he shouted to the man who was roaring abuse at him.

'How's dat, Paul boy?' he shouted back.

'Because you paid to come in to see me.'

On another occasion, Paul was playing outside-right and the crowd were giving him a rough time. The ball was booted across towards the wall on the far side from where we were. Paul was busting a gut trying to get it. He had awful small legs and the crowd on the other side from us were getting it up for him as raced to keep the ball in. He just failed to stop the ball going over the line

The ball hit the wall and came back towards him. Paul drew as if he was going to kick the ball at the crowd. They all ducked. Paul stepped over the ball and gave the crowd, who were still picking themselves up, the two fingers.

We gave him a huge cheer.

There was a junior soccer team in our area called Southern Rovers and they were recruiting for an Under-14 team.

I asked my father if I could join up and he said, 'Go away and play Billy, if you want' even though he was a staunch GAA man.

I was afraid I would be banned from playing GAA if I joined Southern Rovers. In those days, you would be banned from playing GAA if you played soccer or rugby. The County Board sent what were known as 'vigilantes' to the games. These men would then report back to the Board like spies. Of course we were always playing soccer on The Pitch, but that was not an official game, and there was no GAA sanction for playing such games. I still regret I never played soccer with the lads I grew up with.

I will say one thing about Scoil Chríost Rí that still bothers me and that is the soccer players were persecuted. That wasn't right.

Brother Dermot pulled my friend Pat O'Connor out of the line when our class queued up for school in the morning. He gave him a severe grilling and all because Pat was recruiting the boys to play with Southern Rovers. This was a regular occurrence. Another lad, Paddy Murray, got a schoolboy cap for Ireland and was disciplined when he went away to play for his country.

That bias against soccer was not exclusive to Scoil Chríost Rí. It was widespread in nearly all the primary schools. Críost Rí was no different to hundreds of other schools in the times that were in it.

The soccer connection still goes on.

Just before Christmas of 2008 I had a phone call from Tom Coughlan who had bought out Cork City when the club was in financial difficulties.

City are one of the best supported clubs in the League of Ireland and are of course based in Turners Cross, near where I grew up.

'I have a few ideas I want to run by you, Billy. Can we meet?'

I was curious so I met him for a coffee.

Tom offered me the job as manager of Cork City!

I was shocked. Here I was a GAA coach and I was offered the manager's job with one of the best clubs in the league. I did manage a soccer team in the States, but that was years ago and I played well into my forties with my old College friends for Corinthians. I don't think there was a single person in Cork, other than Tom, who saw me as a contender for the City job.

Without really thinking, I told him I would need a coach. Tom mentioned former Blackburn Rovers and Republic of Ireland star Jeff Kenna as my number two. I had no interest in taking the job. I was just curious. I had two other sports jobs to look after.

I told Tom I had already given a commitment to become a selector with the Nemo intermediate footballers and the Nemo junior hurlers.

I think that might have caught Tom by surprise! It was a good call on my part. There were times during the 2009 season when City only barely survived as a club. I still wouldn't have taken the job if City were on a sound financial footing. I had given a commitment to Nemo and that was that as far as I was concerned.

* * *

I was going out to Nemo Rangers at a very early age. Tony played with Nemo and their clubhouse was very near to us. They had a little cabin opposite St Finbarr's Hospital. We listened to Guy Mitchell on the radio in the clubhouse and I seem to remember one song in particular – 'Pretty Little Black-Eyed Suzie' – but the table tennis table was the big attraction.

The green and black jerseys would be hanging out to dry on a line at the back of the shed and all the club's worldly goods such as balls and sliotars were stored in a locked press. Nemo had no pitch of their own back then, as was the case with a good few of the city clubs.

The street league was a great way of getting lads involved with the club from a young age.

The Nemo area was Capwell, Higha, Douglas Street, Turners Cross, Ballyphehane and the Back Douglas Road. Of course Coláiste Chríost Rí was a big Nemo school and some of the Brothers who taught there even played with the club.

We played in the Nemo street leagues in the green in Ballyphehane and we togged out with our own area which was known as Capwell. Connie O'Shea ran our team and how proud he would be to see his son Ciarán now play with the Nemo senior team.

I was about 11 when I started playing Under-15 for Nemo, which was the youngest grade. That was the way it was in those days and I was only one of several 11-year-olds on the team. At the time we were very much a small club with a low profile within the city, even though the big lads won the county junior championship and had gone senior.

Jack Gorman was in charge and he used to call around on his bike to notify us of the matches. Jack brought the jerseys on his bike to the home games and if we were short of players, he used to give kids a tanner or an ice lolly to get them to play. He was the kind of unsung hero who made the GAA what it is today.

I owe him so much.

I had a very happy childhood, but there were times when I felt a little on my own. I suppose it was only natural. I was small and needed a mother. Tony was off in Ballyvourney but Noel, Mary and my dad were always there for me.

Tony always got me to think positively. We had a talk one time in Galway. I'd say I was about 14, which meant Tony was in his early twenties. Now that I think about it, Tony might have suffered from some sort of an inferiority complex himself. He explained to me exactly what an inferiority complex was, as I had never heard of the expression before. He wanted to make sure I had plenty of self-belief. I still think of him and what he said that night, as I did all through my playing career. I think what I got from him was a sense that if you were a good player, or good at anything outside of sport, you didn't have to shout it from the rooftops. Tony said it was important to keep that sense of self-belief inside of you and never to deny it to yourself.

I was very well educated in Scoil Chríost Rí. We weren't whipped or anything and while the likes of Brother Dermot overdid the chastisement, I can't honestly say he left any permanent mark on me. In fact, he was a very good communicator and we did learn an awful lot from him.

Overall, we were very lucky to have received such a fine education. The good far outweighed the bad. There were plenty of games and the teachers gave up much of their free time after school to coach us. The teachers were sincere in their motives. I suppose they were a product of their times.

And of course Small Dan put me on the right road for the coaching and playing of Gaelic football.

I was very lucky to have such a wonderful family. Tonyville was a kid's heaven with no shortage of friends and great neighbours.

My father was a kind man in every way.

# CHAPTER 2

# *Happy Days*

I WENT INTO COLÁISTE CHRÍOST RÍ SECONDARY SCHOOL, BUT IN A WAY I NEVER REALLY LEFT primary school. The first years were installed in a wing of Scoil Chríost Rí, my old primary school building.

Frank Cogan was in the A class with me in first year. Denis Philpott came in from Greenmount and that was the start of a lifetime friendship.

I liked secondary school. We had a different teacher for every class so you weren't stuck all day, every day with someone you might not be getting on too well with and we were allowed a lot more freedom.

In first and second year I was well up there academically, but bit by bit my focus shifted to football and hurling.

We won the Under-17 Dr Rogers Cup when I was in third year.

The corner-back, who happened to be a cousin of our captain and future Cork star John O'Halloran, was giving me a tough time in the semi against Ennis CBS. I pulled around and flaked him with the hurley. Big mistake. He roughed me up and I could do nothing much about it. I was taken off. Brother Denis was our trainer. He was another great man and after he left Críost Rí, he helped in no small way to bring Offaly hurling to the fore.

Brother Denis brought on Paazer Bradley, who was about the same age and size as myself.

'You were a bit too small Bill,' Brother Denis said as I was walking off.

I took fierce umbrage and I said I wasn't going to play anymore. My mind was made up and I wasn't going to change. Retired at 14.

One day after school, Brother Denis had a talk with me.

'You can't give it up Bill,' he said. 'You have to keep going.'

It was lovely stuff. It was man-to-man stuff. Thirty years later that came back to me. You have to deal with fellas man to man, tell it as it is with no lies or excuses. There's no better way with players.

I didn't make it on that team for the final, but I togged out and took my place on the bench without a word. I was very proud of my medal.

Frank and Denis were our leaders and we had a great bunch in the class. Denis died in December 2008 in Kilkenny. We always kept in touch. Denis played in the first Cork minor team to win an All-Ireland football title in 1961. We won two Sigersons together. Denis played Cork senior, but his shoulder kept popping out and that finished his career prematurely.

What a character he was in school and what a fine man he turned out to be.

I was very upset when he died. We met often, but not as often as I would have liked. Now that he has passed on, I greatly regret we didn't spend more time together. He'd come up to Croke Park from Kilkenny with former Cork star Brian Murphy and we'd meet in Ryan's of Parkgate Street. It was as if we were never apart and we fitted into each other's company immediately, just as if we were back in school again.

When I was around 50, there was a special night for John O'Keeffe, a former classmate who was in a wheelchair after falling through a roof. John was a fine hurler and played intermediate for Cork. Denis, Frank and myself were asked to a 'This is Your Life' tribute for John and of course we were only too delighted to attend.

The three of us got talking in my house when the lads called for me and we discussed John's very serious injuries.

Denis was philosophical: 'If we get another 20 years out of life, we'll be doing well.'

I thought, well, we're 50 now and for the first time it dawned on me: life was moving on.

Poor Denis never got to see the 70.

He died of cancer in December 2008. Denis trained Dicksboro and St Kieran's College. A fortnight before he died, he was on the sideline with Dicksboro minors in the county final and he went out the way he lived. Denis, I'm told, got stuck into a linesman and he went on the town with the Dicksboro lads that night even though he was a very sick man.

\* \* \*

I got a respectable enough Inter Cert but I didn't work any harder for the Leaving. If anything, I did even less. I dossed in fifth year and I didn't do much more in Leaving Cert year.

Christmas drifted into Easter and then you're cramming. I did manage to pass the Leaving Cert. I could have gone to university, but my greatest ambition in school was to win a Munster Senior colleges title. I thought if I could graduate with that I would be happy.

We had been showing up well on the way up through the school. We won Under-17 Munster Frewen Cup in football two years in a row. Limerick hurling great Eamonn Cregan and his brother Michael came up against us in one of those campaigns.

I was still young enough to play in the Frewen Cup in Leaving Cert year and I was made captain.

St Brendan's, Killarney beat us in the semi-final. They had some team with the likes of Tony Barrett and Paddy Kennelly, who went on to play for the Kerry minors. Batt O'Keeffe, who went on to become the Minister for Education, was captain and played midfield. I had some great battles with another Kerry minor, Tony Behan, who later became a great friend of mine in university.

I had seen Cork senior club football and the players were much bigger. As a relatively small fella myself, I admired the way Brendan's could fit in small players and feed them with accurate kick passes. Brendan's were beaten in the final but they made a lasting impression on me as to how Gaelic football should be played. There were no football games on TV back in the 1950s and I wasn't exposed to that level of football. Up to then, hurling was my game because I had always seen it played at the very highest level.

The year before we met Brendan's I saw Down beat Kerry in the All-Ireland semi-final in Croke Park.

Down played a more running type of game than Kerry. There was a contrast in styles. Kerry were catch and kick, but I loved that too. I had never seen Gaelic football played with such skill and movement. It was an absorbing game in terms of tactics.

We had a good team in my Leaving Cert year. Frank was captain, but Denis was overage. We lost in the first round of the Munster Senior colleges to DLS Macroom. It was a big shock. I was in the forwards. I hit the post and the ball hit the 'keeper's head with another shot. I couldn't believe it and I took the defeat very badly. For the previous five years I had been looking forward to playing with my school at senior level only to get knocked out in the first round.

I didn't know what to do after the Leaving. I was very young. I told my father I wanted to go back to school to get a few honours, but the reality was I wanted to win a Munster colleges. I went back to school to repeat my Leaving, but I really went back to repeat the Munster Senior colleges.

I was made captain. We went to the semi against De La Salle Waterford, who were hot favourites to win the All-Ireland. We played very well that day. They had the late Eamonn O'Donoghue, who later went on to win All-Irelands with Kerry and became a great friend of mine. Dick Geaney of Castleisland was another star. Jerry Lucey was their full-back and a few years later we played together for Cork. Cavan senior Brendan Murtagh, who was a really special player, also starred for them. I played against Brendan in an All-Ireland senior semi-final in 1967.

Críost Rí played me midfield that day. I gave it everything, but we lost by three points. I would have been underage the following year too, but there was no way I would get away with a third year in Leaving Cert!

My chance of winning a Munster Senior colleges title was gone for good and I was heartbroken.

Mr Daly, who was our maths teacher, must have understood what we were going through. 'Lads,' he said, 'ye have nothing at all to be ashamed of. No team could have tried as hard or put as much into it. Ye just weren't good enough. There's no shame in losing once you give your all.' The man was right. And that was another lesson I learned in Críost Rí.

Hurling was still very much a part of my life – and always will be. I captained the first unbeaten Críost Rí Harty Cup hurling team, well sort of. We were playing St Colman's of Fermoy and we were winning by two points when time was nearly up. Denis was umpire. The sliotar was rolling towards the endline. A Colman's forward was in pursuit and a goal was on. Denis hook-kicked the sliotar over the line before the Colman's boy could get to it and then waved a wide with a great flourish.

The final whistle went a minute later and we won by two points. The referee didn't see Denis kick the sliotar and Colman's subsequently objected. We were instructed to play again. Brother Bonaventure, our principal, refused to play the game.

I was in with a good chance of making the Cork minor hurling team.

Nemo were playing St Michael's in a minor football game and there was a niggle all through even though I wasn't involved at all. There were several fights, but no one was sent off up to then. I was knocked to the ground and one of their players walked on my hand. I got up and hit him and, of course, I got sent off. Just my luck, I missed out on playing with the Cork minor hurlers due to the suspension. Cork played while I was suspended and lost and I was also suspended when Críost Rí won the Simcox Cup final of the Cork colleges in football. It would have been my last game with the school. And, worse again, I would have been captain.

When I look back on it now, the days spent in secondary school in Críost Rí were very happy ones. I didn't win my Munster colleges and I actually did a worse Leaving second time round, but I did get an honour in Irish.

Noel was two classes ahead of me. He always made the school teams and was a great man to look up to. By then Tony qualified as a teacher and he left for London. He came home to visit once or twice a year. Mary still looked after all of us and of course my Dad was as solid as ever.

I played with the Cork minor football team that summer, even though I was suspended for the first game of the championship due to the incident against St Michael's.

I went for a few trials with the footballers when my suspension was lifted and I must have done alright. I was picked at centre half-forward for the Munster Minor final against Kerry in Killarney. I was well used to the Kerry style after playing against St Brendan's and I was confident enough going into the game.

We missed a lot of chances and the match finished in a draw. I did well on the day, but Tony Barrett pulled Kerry back into the game almost on his own.

I got shingles before the replay, but I told no one about it. I felt lousy and, to make matters worse, I was marking Micheál O Sé, the well known commentator, who went on to win two All-Ireland Senior medals with Kerry.

We lost and I didn't do very well.

# CHAPTER 3

## *Off To College – Down The Road*

I STARTED OUT IN UNIVERSITY COLLEGE CORK IN OCTOBER 1963. I DIDN'T HAVE A CLUE WHAT I wanted to do. Eventually I decided to enrol in the three-year BA course. My subjects were Maths, Irish, Geography and Spanish, which I had never heard a word of until my first lecture – I gave no thought whatsoever to my choice of subjects.

It was a complete change from the confinement of secondary school. I was very happy in Críost Rí, but I loved the extra freedom of college life.

I still lived at home in Tonyville and I used to either walk or cycle to the college, which was quite close by.

I didn't play any GAA in first year. I had a few trials, out the field, with College at the start of the year, but I was nowhere near getting on the Sigerson team.

I had a minor altercation with a senior member of Nemo around that time and I developed a bit of a grudge. So I spent the year playing soccer with Tramore Athletic, my local team from Turners Cross. And because of the fact I was a GAA player they played me in goal as the coaches felt my fielding and kicking out of hand would fit the bill nicely for a soccer 'keeper. I had a good few friends in Tramore Athletic, including Pat O'Connor who was chastised in Críost Rí for recruiting for Southern Rovers soccer team.

We won our section of the league and got to the semi of the AOH Cup. I enjoyed my year and I really enjoyed playing in goal. There was more responsibility, like in coming for crosses. I got great satisfaction from commanding the penalty area and controlling the defence, but still all the time at the back of my mind there was the feeling that I should be playing GAA.

I decided to head over to London for the summer and I worked in the tea and biscuits industry, for Lyons Tea and McVities Biscuits. I was paid about £12 a week which wasn't a bad wage at the time. I made enough to cover the fees and to keep myself in college for the next year. There was no free education in those days and most of the students travelled for the summer.

I got the results while I was over there and of course I went down gloriously in the summer exams. It didn't upset me too much.

My brother Tony was in England at the time and I got to spend a lot of time with him, which was great. I enjoyed my summer and went to see a number of soccer games in the old First Division.

I stayed on longer than the rest of the lads. By then I had made up my mind not to repeat the exams.

I had to repeat first year and I took a bit of advice from one of the college wise boys who knew all the tricks of the trade when it came to the exam system. I was advised to keep on Irish and Geography along with what he called a 'kicker' subject. You ditched the kicker at the end of first year. These were easy enough subjects to pass in the exams and so I signed up for Introductory Philosophy. I also took Psychology, a course I was interested in.

When I came back from London, I made up my mind to go back to playing Gaelic football. Someone recommended me to college captain Dave Geaney. Dave was a Kerry senior and a college selector at the time. He asked me to come out and train with UCC. It was as simple as that.

We went on to become lifelong friends. Dave was the first man to pick me as a Gaelic football goalkeeper and nearly 40 years later, he was in the Kerry dressing room when I called in to congratulate them after they beat us in the 2007 All-Ireland final in what turned out to be my last game as Cork manager.

I was picked for the Sigerson panel in November and travelled with the UCC squad to Belfast for the inter-varsity finals.

I had only been in the squad for a few weeks and had never played as a Gaelic football goalkeeper up to that. I was just glad to be on the panel and back playing football. I couldn't believe it when I was picked to play in goal against Queen's University Belfast in the semi-final. Unfortunately, we were well beaten by a very good Queen's team.

It was my first close-up look at Seán O'Neill of Down. O'Neill had been part of an outstanding Down side when the county were the first team ever to bring the Sam Maguire over the border in 1960.

Queen's picked Seán at full-forward. I think it was his first game in the position and he was a revelation. I was mesmerised. O'Neill scored one goal and made the other two by sheer genius. I actually played well and enjoyed the game because I got plenty to do. I was in awe of O'Neill after that match.

Seán didn't just stand at the edge of the square and wait for the high ball to come in. He moved about and was looking to get out in front of his man. O'Neill varied his game and he sometimes moved further out the field and into space. This was a new departure in Gaelic football. Up to then you stayed in your place.

Queen's fed O'Neill with mostly quick, low balls, but he could play it any way it came to him and was well able to mix it too. I started to become aware that you could win games by varying your tactics and although I was totally focused on playing at that time, O'Neill left a lasting impression.

I'll never forget that first Sigerson weekend. It was my first time in Belfast and the northern lads were so thrilled to see us come up. You met lads of your own age from all over Ireland and we made friends in minutes.

My UCC teammates were up for anything. The craic was incredible. Dinny Philpott, my old school pal, was a leading light and had won a county with College in the previous year. There was always a bit of fun and mischief wherever he went.

Dave Geaney was the leader and he looked after me. Dave made sure I was made to feel like one of the lads. I love meeting him to this day – he knows the game better than anyone.

There was no hierarchy in university like we had in secondary school where the first years were at the bottom and the Leaving Cert boys at the top. We were all the same.

It might be years since you last met one of your College teammates, but you can pick it up as if you had been having a kick about with him in the 'Dyke the day before. The Sigerson was really an extension of schools' football which I loved, but we had more freedom and the social side was as good as it gets for any young lad.

I took my first drink that weekend. I drank five bottles of Carlsberg Special. Somehow I got it into my head that Carlsberg Special was a kind of low-level entry into drinking. Nothing could be further from the truth. It was one of the strongest beers on the market. The five bottles blew my head off. We all looked after each other and the lads made sure I came to no harm.

I had two sets of friends by now. There were the college friends and the Tonyville/Nemo pals I grew up with.

I stayed with UCC for the Cork County Championship. The 'College Rule', as it was known as, stated that if you were asked to play with UCC, you had no choice but to play with them. If you refused to play with College and went back to your club, you were banned from lining out in the county championship.

\* \* \*

Dinny McDonnell called to Tonyville around that time to ask if I would go back to Nemo. I hadn't played with Nemo for nearly a year. Dinny was trying to get the struggling Nemo senior football team off the ground.

'Jesus Dinny,' I said, 'it's too late.'

I told him I had just signed for UCC and so I could not play for Nemo, but I was delighted he came to see me.

I passed the exams with flying colours that summer and I even managed to get an honour in Introductory Philosophy which stood me in great stead in my dealings with the Cork County Board over the years. I was getting serious about football again and it was becoming my main focus in life. I was picked on the Cork Under-21 panel and I was up for winning a county championship medal with UCC as we had an even better team than the team that won the year before.

I didn't go to London that summer of 1965. College got to the semi without any great bother and played St Nicholas, or St Nick's, down in the Athletic Grounds. St Nick's were the football wing of the famous Glen Rovers hurling club.

St Nick's were two points up coming up to half-time and we would have a strong breeze in the second half. It was looking good and we were playing well.

Davy Moore, God rest him, was a great character from St Nick's. He shouted out, 'Come on lads, we have 'em.'

I shouted back, 'ya must be joking, Davy boy. We're goin' to destroy ye.'

Not long after that exchange a high ball was flighted back in under the crossbar. I went up for it and two of the Nick's forwards buried me, ball and all, in the back of the net. It should have been a free out, but the green flag went up. The ball was kicked back out and was kicked back in under the crossbar. The same thing happened again and the same two fellas buried me in the back of the net, in exactly the same way. Another goal. Now they were seven points up and we just couldn't catch them in the second half.

I learned two valuable lessons from that day. One was not to be over-confident and the second one was to keep my mouth shut when I was playing The Glen.

\* \* \*

I still had the Cork Under-21s to look forward to.

Kerry were shocked by Clare in the first round which of course left us in a strong position. We beat Clare in the semi and went on to beat Tipp in the final. It was my first Munster medal.

Galway came next in the All-Ireland semi-final at the Athletic Grounds. Galway were hot favourites, but we beat them by three points.

We met Kildare in the final and it was my first time to play in Croke Park which was some thrill. I had been there once before when Kerry met Down, but now here I was playing in an All-Ireland final. Sadly, we were beaten in what was described by the papers as 'one of the best games of football for some time'.

Jack Donnelly, who played senior for Kildare afterwards, let fly with a fine shot from 30 yards out and it dipped under the crossbar. I was off my line, but I didn't let the mistake get me down and just got on with my game.

I was very disappointed as we were sure we would win the All-Ireland. Kildare had a great team with men like Donnelly, Tommy Carew, Pat Dunny and Ollie Crinnigan, who could hold their own at any level.

We had a fine team too, and I think maybe on another day we might have won it. I didn't let the mistake get to me after the match. I was full of confidence in those days and always preferred to catch the ball rather than just punch it out. I had no bother at all in putting mistakes behind me and getting on to the next match. You have to be like that if you are a goalkeeper.

Dr Paddy Fitzgerald was in charge of the UCC teams in those days and that autumn we went straight into training for the Sigerson. Dave Geaney was captain and in Denis Leahy we had a superb physical trainer who was years ahead of his time. Denis introduced us to circuit training and even though he was quietly spoken, the players really responded to him.

It was 13 years since we last won the Sigerson.

UCC started to recruit players. Mick Morris, the Kerry senior centre half-back, was brought in from his job in Claremorris with the ESB and was signed up to do a night course. Frank Cogan and Cork full-back Jerry Lucey were registered as rural science students. At least Frank had played the year before and Jerry was from Cork, but Mick had no connection with UCC.

And while the rules probably weren't broken, they were certainly stretched to the limits. We were up against the system anyway.

UCD were the host college that year. The rules were weighted very much in favour of the home university. Amazingly, they could pick not only their own referees, but also their own semi-final opponents. They chose us in the belief we were the weakest team in the competition. That suited us down to the ground and we used their assessment of us as a team to motivate ourselves.

We stayed in the Lucan Spa and that was the first time we met Mick Morris. He sat down for tea with us and it was as if he knew us all his life.

We won with a point from Dave in the seventh minute of injury time. We took on University College Galway in the final. They were hot favourites and were backboned by Pat Donnellan, Enda Colleran and Liam Sammon from the great Galway three-in-a-row team. That game was played the following day and we hosed them by 3-9 to 0-5.

We had an absolute ball. We had a right slag off the UCD boys at the Sigerson dinner that night. Geaney kept on saying 'ye picked the plugs' during the speeches and that team became known among ourselves as 'The Plugs'. 'Plug' was a goofy cartoon character who was famed for getting everything wrong.

We celebrated for weeks afterwards and it didn't do my studies much good, but there was never a dull moment. Someone even composed a song to the air of 'The Patriot Game'.

> *'Come all ye young students and list while I sing,*
> *For the love of one's college is a terrible thing.*
> *It banishes fear with the speed of a flame,*
> *And makes us all part of the Sigerson Game.'*

# CHAPTER 4

# *On The Up And Up*

THAT SIGERSON WIN WAS IN NOVEMBER 1965 AND SHORTLY AFTERWARDS I WAS CALLED IN to the Cork senior panel for the National League.

Limerick had beaten Cork the year before in the first round of the Munster Championship and there were calls for changes to the set-up. Several of the team that reached the final of the Under-21 championship were called into the squad.

Cork legends Eamonn Young, Weesh Murphy and Donie O'Donovan, or Donie Donovan as we called him, took over the team that year. These were men you could look up to and it was a great vote of confidence to get on their panel. I didn't get any run in the league, but I did make my Cork senior debut in a challenge game against Offaly in Tullamore on Easter Sunday, 1966.

And I was involved on and off with the senior team, in one way or another, for the next 41 years.

I didn't do anything wrong in the Easter Sunday challenge, and at least I didn't play myself off the team in my first game. My abiding memory is leaving the Cork dressing room with my very good friend, the late Mickey Buckley from Ballincollig. We were the last two out of the changing room and we stopped to comb our hair in the reflection of the window of the Offaly dressing room – it must have been considered unmanly to have mirrors in GAA dressing rooms in those days. We spotted the Offaly jerseys thrown down on the ground and we took two as souvenirs of our first outing with the seniors. I suppose I was always a bit of a hoarder. I still have that jersey and I have no notion of giving it back.

I held my place in the Cork team for the championship against Clare. We played very well. The management team brought a special atmosphere into the camp and I was very confident going into my first Munster Senior final against Kerry, who had been beaten in the two previous All-Ireland finals by a superb Galway team.

The game was played in Killarney and I had a good idea what to expect from my minor days.

I made a couple of great saves in the first half and we were winning comfortably when Tony Barrett came on as a sub for Kerry. He was the same Tony Barrett who changed the course of the Munster minor final three years previously.

I jumped up for a high ball and Tony fisted it to the back of the net. That brought it down to a goal and we had a nervous last few minutes, but we held on. It was our first Munster final win in nine years. Cork football was on the up and up. We had a succession of good underage teams and, best of all, we beat Kerry on their home ground in Killarney.

We came up against Galway in the All-Ireland semi-final a few weeks later. They had won the previous two All-Irelands and were rightly considered to be one of the greatest teams of all time. We matched them all the way and that was without a doubt Cork's best ever performance of that era.

We missed two goal chances and Cyril Dunne scored one for Galway. They were a point up with two minutes to go. I was playing in the Canal End goal and I can see it right now. Jerry Lucey, our full-back, chased Cyril out towards the Cusack Stand.

Eamon Mowles from Wicklow gave Galway what I thought was a ridiculous free and from the free Cyril floated it over the bar.

We might have made a draw out of it if that free hadn't been awarded. I felt especially sorry for Jerry ,who was a mighty man to have in front of you. He always backed me up in the early days and he was badly wronged that day.

Galway went on to beat Meath in the final and complete the three-in-a-row. Johnny Geraghty was their goalkeeper and at the time he was the best in the country. He was so agile and quick. Up to then Gaelic 'keepers might be safe, but he brought the game to a new level with diving for the ball and picking out his man from his clearances.

Galway and Geraghty set the standard for all of Ireland for the previous three years and we gave a very good account of ourselves. We had a good set-up and the future looked bright.

Donie fixed me up with a job down Centre Park Road in the construction of the new Dunlop building. I was only a few hundred yards from the Athletic Grounds where we did most of our training and I earned enough for the following year in college. It was typical of Donie. He did everything he could to make for a good atmosphere and was clever enough to see the bigger picture.

We used to go down to the Queen's Hotel after training for milk and sandwiches. It was owned by a great old Cork hurler called Johnny Quirke, and his wife Hannah.

Mikey was the head waiter in the Queen's and he used to do everything. Someone might shout 'Mikey, bring us a few more sandwiches', and Mikey would run into the kitchen to make the sandwiches. He might be after bringing in a bucket of coal a few minutes earlier and there would be black smudges from his hands on the white sliced bread. There was a waitress there who had huge boobs, and one of the lads used to say to her, 'I'd love to...' and she'd say 'will ya go 'way boy, you'd need a bunch of 'em.'

On Wednesday nights in the Queen's you were allowed two drinks a man courtesy of the Cork County Board. Now you could have orange or lemonade or a couple of pints. No one ever missed training on Wednesdays.

The older fellas might just have the sandwiches and the milk and we often invited our buddies in on the Wednesday nights and passed them off as Cork footballers. We would drink five or six pints and we brought Mikey onside from the outset. The call would be 'Mikey, two more pints there. And Mikey, a small one for yourself'.

And Mikey would have a small one for himself. And then when our quota was used up, we went down to the Arcadia ballroom for the Wednesday night dance. It all added to the camaraderie and win, lose or draw, we went back to the Queen's for chicken and ham after the matches. And, of course, the 'two' pints.

\* \* \*

It was back to College in October of 1966 for my degree year.

Dinny Philpott, my old classmate, was made UCC captain and Mick Morris got to like us so much, he was now in College full-time. The team that went up to Galway for the Sigerson that year was totally legit.

We played UCG, the hosts, in the final. We were level coming up to half-time and were doing very well after playing against a strong breeze.

Up to then, everything went in the Sigerson. You could do anything bar murder. Dinny clocked one of the UCG boys and was sent to the line by future GAA President, Dr Mick Loftus. Dr Loftus also sent Dinny's brother Eric off for what Cork people considered to be a harmless offence in the 1964 All-Ireland Minor final. And so Dinny became the first man ever to get sent off in a Sigerson.

Dinny was in a terrible state in the dressing room at half-time. He stood up on the seat and with the tears streaming down his face, he begged us to do it for him.

'Lads – f**k sake,' he said, in his strong Cork accent, 'I know I left ye down, but please lads, please lads. Jesus, please lads – will ye do it for me.'

We all loved that man and we beat a very good UCG team with 14 men. We won it by a point and it was significant that it was Eric Philpott who kicked the winning score.

And of course being young and foolish, we got into a bit of bother that night in Eyre Square when Eric showed us how he kicked the winning point using the Sigerson Cup as a ball.

Then there was the game I had been dreading. UCC drew Nemo in the Cork County championship. I went in to that game with mixed feelings. I saved a penalty from my very good friend John McCarthy, and we won easily enough.

We played Carbery in Kinsale in the county semi-final near the end of the year. Both teams togged off in a certain Murphy's Hotel and it was there I met my future wife Mary, Mary Allen as she was then, for the second time.

I met her a week earlier at a rugby dance in Cork Con and took her out to dance, but that was as far as it went.

Some one of the lads told me there were ten daughters in Murphy's Hotel and every one of them was better looking than the next. And who should be there by complete chance only Mary.

We got on fine and I took her to the dance in Kinsale that night. I was wearing my UCC tie and, if I say so myself, I was looking my best.

I did a bit of work in my degree year and duly passed first time out in the summer exams.

# CHAPTER 5

## *The Punch That Wasn't*

**DONIE O'DONOVAN TOOK OVER FULL TRAINING OF THE CORK FOOTBALL TEAM HALF-WAY** through the 1967 season. Eamonn Young, who was joint trainer, went away on overseas duty with the Irish Army leaving Donie in sole control. At this stage we had grown very fond of Donie. If he said to us, 'jump off the County Hall', we'd have done it.

We met Kerry in the Munster final in the old Athletic Grounds. There was no mercy in Kerry-Cork games.

The late Thorny O'Shea, the Kerry corner-forward, was clocked as the ball was thrown in. I wouldn't agree with that and it's something I wouldn't have been very proud of as a Corkman. You wouldn't mind a row that breaks out spontaneously or retaliation if you were being blackguarded, but this was premeditated. I have always been that way, whether it was Kerry or Cork, or anyone else who got up to dirty play.

It was tit-for-tat all through and there was no holding back. That was one of my best games for Cork. I made a save from DJ Crowley and it was from point-blank range. I dived full-length and managed to fingertip the ball away. I was delighted with myself. DJ had a powerful shot and later went on to score one of the greatest goals of all time in an All-Ireland final.

Eamonn O'Donoghue was in goal for Kerry that day and he was brought out the field to take a free to make a draw out of it with a minute to go. The free was from way out on the left. I remember the ball turning, turning and eventually it went inches wide. Game over. We won it by a point.

We walked through the crowd in our gear to get to the cars and drove back to Cook Street in the city centre where we togged off in the Cork County Board rooms. Our dressing rooms in the old Athletic Grounds were a disaster. The showers were cold, the water was only a trickle and the place was filthy.

The Cork supporters clapped us all the way until we got out to the car park. The Kerry players trailed out after us through the mixed ranks of Cork and Kerry supporters. I can't think of a better way to leave the ground after beating Kerry.

We had become the first Cork team to beat Kerry two years in a row. We didn't realise this until after the game when we were told about it in a pub and of course that made the win all the sweeter.

We beat Cavan in the All-Ireland semi but were extremely lucky to win by a point. We got two soft goals. The first goal came when the ball bounced over the goalkeeper's head and the second came from a penalty when one of their backs dived on the ball. There was a feeling of anti-climax after beating Kerry. You built yourself up to knock Kerry out and that in itself was a kind of an All-Ireland. This was always a problem for Cork teams, but at least we won and I was in my first All-Ireland final against Meath.

We were quietly confident going up in the train as we had beaten Meath well the year before in the Grounds Tournament. There was a big crowd of Cork supporters there to meet us off the train. It was Cork's first football final in ten years and most people felt we were in with a very good chance of winning.

We were all over Meath in the first half, but we only led by three points at half-time. Meath almost failed to score in that first half. Years later, I listened to a tape recording of the Mícheál O'Hehir commentary of the game.

'It looks like for the first time ever a team will fail to score in the first half of an All-Ireland final.'

Meath scored just before half-time and we went in leading by 0-4 to 0-1. We left it after us in that first half. Cork should have been ten points up at half-time, but we missed score after score.

We were still leading by that three points until Meath were awarded a 14-yard free early in the second half. Tony Brennan was their free-taker and six or seven players lined the goal. Normally you would expect a near-in free to go over the bar, but Tony failed to rise the ball and Jerry Lucey booted his clearance well out the field. Matty Kerrigan kicked it back in.

The Meath and Cork players ran out from the goal, all bar Meath's Terry Kearns who was knackered and was hunched over with his hands on his knees.

Terry jumped up when he saw the ball coming in. I knew he was there and I spotted him coming in from my right-hand side. I was first out to the ball. My first thought was to knock it away, but just as the ball came to me at the last second, I changed my mind and tried to catch it. Terry, fair play to him, got a knuckle to the ball and it glanced over my right shoulder and into the net.

I was disgusted. That goal put them level and they tacked on a few more points after that. We had more chances to win it and we gave it everything but Meath won by three points.

I was distraught after the match.

Hal O'Brien was first out on the pitch to console me. We were great friends, grew up together and continued the friendship in College.

I just pushed him away. I didn't want to talk to anyone. If only I hadn't changed my mind and punched it away, we might have been All-Ireland champions. It still goes through my head and again I can picture it right in front of me.

I didn't enjoy the after-match dinner in the Green Isle Hotel. The food was fine, but we were split and put sitting at tables with the guests. I was sick of the match by now. There were fellas at the table who were talking about the game and blaming this fella and that fella. I was the only player at the table and I couldn't take anymore so I left with Hal, who was there for me again at the dinner. That was the difference between friends and hangers-on. The friends were there when you were beaten.

We had a few drinks back at the hotel and spent most of Monday drinking as well.

Then on the Tuesday after the All-Ireland final we hit off for Listowel races. It was great to get out of Cork and away from all the post-mortems.

We were looking forward to cutting loose. Inter-county players give up so much of their free time and have to condense a summer's socialising into a few days.

I travelled down with my good friends Eric Philpott, Kevin Dillon and Johnny Carroll who were on the Cork team that lost the final.

I was dying on the way down to Listowel. I thought it was the effects of the hangover from the booze-up after losing the All-Ireland. The lads put it down to the fact that I wasn't used to drinking. My stomach was killing me and Kevin Dillon gave me a brandy and port by way of a 'cure'.

I must have been in a bad way because I left Listowel races and went back home to Cork.

I was sent for tests and I was diagnosed with mononucleosis, which is some sort of liver ailment. I was in hospital for a fortnight and missed the county final against Beara from West Cork.

The game finished in a draw and I was allowed out to see the match, but it was straight back into hospital afterwards. I was out for the replay, but I wasn't allowed to play. We lost by a couple of points to a fine Beara team.

I was very sick and it took me a while to get over the mononucleosis.

At least I was cleared to play football and played in the Sigerson again which was moved to January due to an outbreak of foot and mouth disease.

Denis Philpott became the second man to get sent off in a Sigerson in the semi after only five minutes when he clocked an opponent. It was Moss Keane's first Sigerson and he played at full-back. Moss was a very quiet fella, but as the game went on he grew more and more passionate. Joe McLoughlin, the UCG full-forward, was as big as Moss and they were having a fierce battle.

Moss pointed to the 21-yard line and said to Joe 'if you come inside that line, I'll kill you'. And the way he said it, you'd take heed.

We were eventually beaten by a point. And that night we cut loose after weeks of abstinence.

The Sigerson dinner was held in Wynns Hotel, just off O'Connell Street, and the hotel closed the bar due to over-exuberance. There were lads standing up on top of tables, throwing pints over each other and the different colleges were vying with each other to see who could cause the most mayhem.

Big Moss was standing up at the bar and there was no way he would ever throw away a pint. We noticed he had a full glass.

'Where's the bartender gone?' we asked Moss.

'How would I know? It's giving me all I can do to keep an eye on ye lot.'

Moss asked us if we would have a drink. Now Moss was as decent a man as ever walked, but none of us could afford to go buying big rounds of drink. And anyway, how could we when the bar staff had disappeared?

And that was the introduction of the American-style pitchers of beer to Ireland. Moss stretched out over the counter and filled a water jug with beer. He topped us up and soon half the bar was getting served by Moss. There was no shortage of drink after that, but eventually the bar staff copped on and we were all fecked out.

I can also say I played with Moss in his first ever rugby game. There was a game between Bill Ludgate's, which was mainly a GAA bar, and The Star, which was mainly a rugby bar. I played outhalf and scored a drop goal from 40 yards out. Moss didn't have much of a clue about the rules and he as he often said himself, he didn't take much notice of them at any stage of his career. At one stage he even soloed the ball.

Derry Crowley, the owner of The Star, put up two barrels and by the end of the night, the drop goal was 80 yards out. Moss was second-row along with the equally big Pat O'Meara. Moss caught a ball in the lineout and charged up the field with half the Star team hanging off him. He was a colossus. Derry later spent an hour trying to persuade Moss to play rugby, but Moss took no notice and he didn't take up the game seriously until a year or two after that.

There are so many stories about Moss that it's hard to separate the truth from the fiction. There was the day I saw him stuck in the schoolboys' turnstile outside Flower Lodge when he tried to bluff his way in. O'Meara and himself used to co-own a Fiat 500. There wasn't enough leg room so they took out the front seat and drove it from the back seat.

Moss is a very intelligent man and could easily have taken the academic route.

I was so proud when he played for Ireland and Munster. We had a few pints together after Munster beat the All Blacks in 1978 and we have always been the best of friends. He is basically a shy man, but he has a brilliant sense of humour and is as fine a man as I have ever met. Moss is fighting a battle with cancer. He is always in good form, and every now and then I say a little prayer he will be alright. No better man.

I took my first steps into management around then when I became Dinny Philpott's assistant. Dinny was appointed manager of the UCC Freshers or first year team. We had Brendan Lynch on that team as captain and he went on to win several All-Irelands with Kerry.

Dinny had a great way with the players and I learned a lot from him. We went on to win the competition out.

\* \* \*

I was teaching for a few hours a week as part of my H Dip course in the Cork Tech and the Cork 'one day a week'.

I really enjoyed 'the one day a week'. The kids were working as Echo boys (selling papers) or as messenger boys but by law they had to go to school one day a week. I was only a few years older than some of the one day a week boys and I got on great with them.

It wasn't as strict as Cork Tech and one day when I was only a few weeks in the job, John D Hickey, who was one of the top GAA journalists in the country with 'The Irish Independent', came to the school to interview me. It was just before the 1967 All-Ireland final. There were books, paper planes and rubbers flying around the classroom when John D came in to the class. The lads were running around the room and John D was genuinely shocked, but he didn't write about it in his article.

I enjoyed my time there. There was no great harm in the lads who were as bright as any I came across in later years, but didn't get the chances the kids get now to further their education. Jerry Myers was in my first class and he was no bother. Jerry went on to play with Cork Celtic afterwards and we are good friends to this day.

I trained as much as I could in that H Dip year, but I never attended a single lecture. I passed the practical which was based on teaching ability and I expected to pass the written exams without any great difficulty. Nobody ever failed the Dip back in those days.

I went up to the college to get my results which were posted up for all to see on the arched entrance to the older part of the university known as The Quad.

I was at the back of a mob of students who were looking for their names on the board. If your name wasn't up on the board, it meant you failed.

Then I heard this loud voice.

'Do ya know who didn't get it at all?' a girl said to her friend. 'Who?' asked the pal.

'Billy Morgan,' replied the girl shouting back to her pal.

I slunk away from the back of the crowd, hoping no one would recognise me and got out of the college grounds as quickly as I could. I repeated the Dip in the autumn and I only did a little bit more work as I was busy training and working on the buildings.

We were given exactly the same paper as the one we were given in the summer and this time I passed.

And that was it. My five years in UCC had come to an end and I have to say that, apart from the occasional lapse in exams, I enjoyed every minute of it.

Of course I was still playing away with Cork during the summer of 1968.

We beat Clare in the first round of the championship up in Ennis and we were haunted to get out of it. We won by a point.

Clare got a penalty with about five minutes to go. We were three points up. Someone went down injured and there was a bit of a delay. A spectator came down off the terrace at the back of the goal and on to the pitch. The goals were like the tide had just gone out and the spectator grabbed a fistful of sand and threw it in my face.

He ran away and I lost the head. I went to run after him and Patsy Harte, our corner-back, stopped me as I went running round the goalpost.

'Don't worry, Billy,' said Patsy. 'I have him. I have him. Easy goes Bill. Easy Bill. Take it handy Bill. Calm down.'

I was livid but Patsy wouldn't let me up into the terrace at the back of the goal. He just held on to me and if he said 'easy Bill' once, he said it ten times. Patsy was perfectly calm throughout. He never took his eyes of the sand-thrower who was making his way back up the terraces.

'I have him,' he said as the sand-thrower settled himself about three or four rows up. Patsy walked calmly up the terrace and clocked the sandman.

Clare scored the penalty but we went back down the field and got the winning point in injury time.

We played Kerry yet again in the final and there was controversy before that game as well. Nemo were playing in the county championship just a few weeks before the Munster final and there was a flare-up on the line. I think an umpire might have got a belt. The upshot of the inquiry was that Frank Cogan was suspended for six months. Now I wasn't playing that day – I was still with College – but in my opinion Frank was completely innocent of any wrongdoing.

Nemo were very bitter over the incident. Some of the Cork fans threw sods at a member of the Cork County Board as he came out on to the pitch in Fitzgerald Stadium.

Mick O'Connell and Mick O'Dwyer came out of retirement for the championship and there was massive interest in that game.

Another Kerry star, the ever-dependable Johnny Culloty, came back in goal, but we started brilliantly and went into a seven-point lead with goals from two young lads, Ray Cummins and Donal Hunt. Then the great Mick O'Connell took over and Kerry wiped us out. The final score was 1-21 to 3-8.

O'Connell was one of the purest footballers I ever saw. He ran the show. His fielding was immaculate. His kick passing was incredible. The Kerry style has always been labelled catch and kick, but it should be named 'catch and kick accurately'. O'Connell developed that style and was its finest exponent. That day I couldn't help but admire him. Mick O'Dwyer kicked points from all angles and my friend Eamonn O'Donoghue scored a great goal near the end – just when I thought we had kept Kerry from hitting the net. Even still, that was one of my better games for Cork.

Cork had been to the All-Ireland semi-final in 1966, running a famous Galway team very close. We reached the All-Ireland final the following year and even though we were beaten, we were far from disgraced.

We definitely weren't the same team in 1968 and there were some selections which didn't help either. I was very frustrated.

Donie Donovan pulled out after a hurling game between UCC and the Glen when severe sanctions were imposed on the Glen. The Glen withdrew from the championship and all of their players left the county panels. That left Nemo and the Glen in conflict with the County Board and it was definitely unsettling, to say the very least.

I spent the rest of the summer working on a building site out in Togher. Donie – who else? – fixed me up with a job. That was another thing about that man. He would do his best to help you out if you were stuck and he had very good contacts all over the city.

I used the money I earned on the buildings to pay off my student loans. I am still paying them off!

# CHAPTER 6

# *Behind Enemy Lines*

**I FOUND IT VERY HARD TO GET USED TO THE REAL WORLD AFTER FIVE YEARS IN COLLEGE, BUT** I had to face into getting a job as a teacher after getting the Dip in the autumn of 1968. It wasn't easy to get a job in those days, and I had no luck at all in Cork.

There was talk of a teaching post in Birr, Co Offaly. Birr was a long way from home and it would be very difficult to get to and from training.

As I weighed up my options, the good life went on a while longer and a gang of us went down to the Listowel races. I met the Leahy family from Market Street in the town at the races and they were a great GAA family. There were four Leahy brothers – Eamonn, Tadhg, John and Gerard, who were all very good players. Their parents Eddie and Sheila put me in touch with Patsy O'Sullivan who was the principal of Causeway Comprehensive, a new school about 17 miles from Listowel.

Patsy was a GAA man and he offered me a job. By then, the Offaly job had come through, but Kerry was handier for training. I was delighted. I came down to Listowel for the races and went back with a job. The previous year I went home with a dose of mononucleosis.

It was my first time leaving home. I had this terrible lonesome feeling as I came down in the bus to Tralee. I was putting college life behind me and I was facing into a new life and a new job. I was always a home bird and Cork was the only place I ever wanted to live. I had good friends like Dave Geaney from college, but he was in Castleisland, which was a good bit away from Listowel, and I had no car.

Sheila Leahy told me I could stay with her for a few days until I got fixed up with a place of my own. I ended up staying with the Leahys for the rest of the year I spent in Kerry. It was a home away from home.

Sheila used to drive into Tralee to pick me up off the bus and I could come and go as I pleased.

Gerald McKenna was the vice-principal in Causeway and he became a great friend of mine. Gerald later went on to become chairman of the Kerry County Board during the Golden Years. He really looked after me. There was always a word of advice if needed and both he and Patsy couldn't have treated me better if I was on the Kerry team.

Eamonn O'Donoghue was another pal. Poor Eamonn died a young man and we used to pal around a fair bit and travelled to and from matches together. I was also very friendly with Eamonn's brother Paudie who sadly died in recent years.

Eamonn and myself were on the Munster Railway Cup team that year I was living in Listowel. I would say, no more than myself, he was only just getting used to the transition from student life. We failed to get out of Dublin on the Sunday night of the Railway Cup match.

The following morning I phoned Gerald McKenna.

'I'm still in Dublin,' I said to my boss.

'Don't worry about that,' he replied. 'I'll look after your classes.'

Gerald lived in Ballyduff and we'd often stop there for a pint on our way home to Listowel. He had a great turn of phrase and I could listen to him all day and night. Andy Molyneaux also taught in Causeway. He later became secretary of the Kerry County Board and Andy was another man who was very good to me in my first year out.

We were always talking about GAA in the staff room and when we played Kerry in the National League, Mick O'Connell lobbed me. The boys let me know all about it. I was very happy in Causeway at the school and in Listowel where I lived. I would never have left it, but for the football. There was never any bother in the school. I got on very well with all the kids and the teachers.

Gerard was the youngest of the Leahys and he looked upon me as a big brother. He was in first year when I arrived and we became very close. We played ball all the time.

I was the only one at home with Gerard; the lads were working outside of Kerry. Gerard went on to win two All-Ireland Under-21 medals with Kerry and was on the senior panel until he emigrated to the United States in the early 1980s.

I used to go down to John B Keane's pub in Listowel and we'd have a pint during the week. We chatted away about most things and we became great friends. We kept up the friendship right up until John B's death in May 2002.

Donal Lenihan's dad Gerard used to bring me home to Cork. Gerard was a Listowel man who played with Nick's in his younger days and you wouldn't feel the journey going with him.

I came from a city where the big sports were hurling and soccer, but everything in Kerry was geared towards football and the county team.

I trained very hard. During the winter, I trained in the Listowel GAA pitch. I used to kick the ball off the wall there which was uneven. The ball came back at different angles and it was a great way of keeping the reflexes sharp.

There was a street light which lit up the area where I trained. Gerard Leahy would come up with me. And after training we would call to Roly Chute for sausages and chips. That was the highlight for Gerard, but I wonder what the modern-day nutritionists would think of that? There were a few pints with Eamonn 'Bomber' O'Connor and the Listowel Emmets lads in Mike the Pie's which was owned by the Bomber's dad.

No one ever had a go at me over being from Cork. It was an ideal existence.

We came up against Kerry in the semi-final of the league while I was still teaching in Causeway.

We played them off the field for most of the match, but Liam Higgins scored a goal with just a few minutes to go and Kerry won by two points. The ball hit a post and sneaked over the line. I was in a desperate state. There was no way we deserved to lose that match.

Mícheál Ó Muircheartaigh approached me as I was coming off the pitch. He picked a bad time to come over to interview me. I was never easy to talk to in the immediate aftermath of a defeat.

'Billy, did ye think ye were unlucky?'

'Unlucky,' I replied in a high-pitched voice that seems to come on me when I get mad.

'People might say that Cork were unlucky to concede a last-minute goal.'

'Unlucky,' I screeched back at Mícheál.

'We can take it so Billy you felt Cork were unlucky?'

'Unlucky,' I screamed back again.

And that was the end of the interview. I wasn't able to do the standard answers. Years later, I was at the UCC dinner and all the lads slagged me off with 'unluckys' coming at me every five minutes. And Páidí ó Sé has a hop-ball off me every time we meet.

Dr Con Murphy, the Cork team doctor, milked that story over the years and sometimes when he meets me he doesn't say hello, he says 'unlucky'.

\* \* \*

I was up and down to Cork all the time that year. By now I was back playing football with Nemo, but that didn't stop me going to the Sigerson Cup to support the boys.

My Kerry friends didn't show us any mercy in that year's Munster final. We were hammered by 0-16 to1-3. Kerry were all over us, but at least I didn't give away a goal. It was probably my greatest game for Cork and the save I made from Liam Higgins with about five minutes to go was also my best ever.

And once again I got a close-up view of one of my all-time heroes, Mick O'Connell. As we kicked the ball around before the match at the Blackrock end of the old Athletic Grounds, Kerry swept onto the field past us. There was a huge roar as O'Connell came prancing onto the pitch and it sent a shiver down my spine.

I was in awe of him to a certain extent.

Kerry got a free 60 yards out in that final and he put it straight over the bar, but for some reason the referee called it back. Micko put the ball down in exactly the same spot and kicked it straight over the bar. Sheer genius.

# CHAPTER 7

# *A Grand Old Team to Play For*

IT WAS TURNING OUT TO BE AN EVENTFUL YEAR. SHORTLY AFTER THE 1969 MUNSTER FINAL, a man named Billy Hardy called to my house and asked if I was interested in going to Glasgow Celtic on trial.

Now Celtic were the best side in Europe at the time. They had won the European Cup two years previously in one of the great finals against Inter Milan in Lisbon and I was a big Celtic fan.

Billy used to call to the house nearly every day. Billy was a grand fella, but the whole saga dragged on so long I was beginning to doubt if anything would ever come of it.

One weekend we went down to Listowel to visit the Leahys on the back of Mickey Bawn Flynn's scooter. Mickey later did the physical training with Kilkenny and was Irish Triple Jump champion. While we were there, Billy Hardy contacted Leahys and asked would I be able to go to Celtic Park in the morning.

So it was back up to Cork from Listowel, from there to Dublin and then across to Glasgow. Billy travelled with me.

We were met by Seán Fallon, who was the assistant manager of Celtic at the time and a Sligo man. Seán had always been interested in Gaelic football and played for his local club, Craobh Rua.

Seán played with Celtic for many years and took over as Jock Stein's assistant when he gave up playing. He was surprised to see us.

'I told ye to ring me when ye were coming over. We're playing our most important match of the year tonight.'

It was the night of the Celtic-Rangers Old Firm derby. It seems Seán told Billy to bring me over and Billy just went off and organised everything without finalising the details with Seán. I was mortified.

Celtic put us up in a hotel and we watched the game which Celtic won 1-0. The atmosphere was incredible. The singing of political songs and the open hostility between the two sets of supporters caught me by surprise. I fell in love with the place that night. What started out as 'a we'll see how things will work out' jaunt, had changed into a serious option for me.

I stayed in the house next door to Seán Fallon and travelled to training with him every day. We got on very well together. Seán was a lovely man and I think he had good time for me as a player.

I trained with the Celtic first team from the beginning. I was in Listowel with my pals just a few days earlier and here I was with the Lisbon Lions that won the European Cup. We walked from Parkhead up to the training ground in Barrowfield. We carried a ball each and there was good bit of chat. The Celtic players made me very welcome. There were no egos there.

Jock Stein, the Celtic manager, took most of the sessions. I remember doing this shooting drill in front of my goal. Tommy Gemmell shot and I dived, but got nowhere near the ball. In fact, I didn't even see it until I turned around to pick it out of the net.

Gemmell came over to me and said, 'Don't worry son. I've beaten the best goalkeepers in Europe'.

Billy McNeill, who was captain of the club, was very encouraging to me. Bertie Auld would come up and ask how I was getting on.

I played in one full game. Davie Cattanach came down the right wing and got me inside the near post. Goalkeepers should never get caught at the near post. Then he did it to me again! It was meant as a cross, but he didn't catch it right and I was at the far post waiting to grab the high ball.

Kenny Dalglish turned around and said, 'Did that go in?' Didn't I feel silly then? Lou Macari, Danny McGrain, and David Hay played in that game. They were gifted players. Strangely, I didn't feel overawed. I was always quiet and a little bit too shy for my own good, but I didn't feel out of place. And I always thought of my brother Tony's words all those years ago when he told me to have confidence in myself.

Before I left for Scotland I was offered a full-time teaching job back in Cork. I was in a dilemma as the Celtic trial was for a month and if I stayed, I would lose the job which was due to start the following Monday. I explained my situation to Seán.

Jobs were scarce back then. A job in Cork would be ideal for going to training. I was always a Corkman first and foremost and loved living in the city.

Seán said he couldn't give me any guarantees whether or not they would sign me at the end of the month. That was fair enough. I thought about it for a while and then I told him I was going back to Cork.

'Why don't you come back over again at Christmas during your school holidays? In the meantime, we will come over to see you.'

I left at the end of the week and started work as a teacher in St John's Technical School the following Monday. Then around October I got a letter from Celtic informing me they had signed Evan Williams from Wolves and there was no need to come back.

That season Celtic reached the European Cup final again only to be beaten by Feyenoord of Holland and Evan Williams played in that match. I often wondered what would have happened if I had stayed for the month.

Could it have been me who played in that European Cup final? Would I have made it? Who knows? I have no regrets.

# CHAPTER 8

## *Strawberry Fields*

**AFTER THE HIGHS OF GLASGOW, I WAS SOON BROUGHT BACK DOWN TO EARTH.**

Back in Cork and teaching in St John's, I was playing with Nemo now and who should we come up against in the Cork County Championship only College. Now if the previous year's Munster final was one of my best games, that semi against College was definitely my worst. Even now the thought of it puts me in bad form.

I conceded two terrible goals. The first was when I was soloing out with the ball and was looking up for someone to pass to. I went to punt it out, but I kicked the ground and it dribbled out to Ray Cummins, my future brother-in-law. Ray passed it to Brendan Lynch who stuck it in the back of the net.

Dinny McDonnell was playing full-back that day for Nemo and he scrambled to get back to help me out. Dinny broke his leg and that injury more or less finished his playing career. I felt absolutely terrible about that.

Then after that disaster, I let in another bad goal as well. Nemo gave College a great game of it too and would probably have beaten them but for the two soft goals I gave away.

Cork played Tipp in the 1970 Munster semi in Clonmel and we had no trainer. We beat them in Clonmel, but we were lucky.

Babs Keating, who was a fine footballer as well as a great hurler, starred that day. We escaped with a last-minute goal.

One of the former Cork greats came to the game with a view to taking over as trainer. He mustn't have liked what he saw because he told us he didn't have the time to train us.

Denis Leahy was doing the physical training with us by then and he was excellent. We did our best to get ourselves going. But we were basically left to our own devices by the County Board.

Surprise, surprise. We were well beaten by Kerry and they went on to win their second successive All-Ireland .

\* \* \*

I left for Strawberry Hill in September of 1970. We were the second batch of PE teachers to be sent to England while the government was building Thomond College. Mary and myself got engaged on the eighth of September, shortly before I left for England.

In Strawberry Hill, we were taught how to teach all sorts of sports. I never minded the study. It was sports full-time and I was sports-mad. I loved the practical aspect of it. We could be out on the pitch for soccer training at nine in the morning, and it felt like as if we were full-time professional sportsmen.

By now, I had it in my head, that some day I would train Gaelic football teams. I learned an awful lot about training teams in Strawberry Hill. Up to then Gaelic football training consisted of a few sprints and a few laps of the pitch. Strawberry Hill concentrated on the Five S's: speed, strength, skill, stamina and soul. There was a big emphasis too on flexibility.

I used the drills I learned all through my career. We had very good coaches there and I adapted soccer drills to GAA in later years.

I came back home to play with Nemo in the final of the county against Muskerry and coming up to half-time we were six points up. Straight after half-time, a very young Dinny Allen scored another goal to put us nine points up. I then let in three goals. I didn't play particularly well in the first year or two after I went back to Nemo.

I was coming around the post to collect one ball and I totally misjudged it. The ball hit the post and the Muskerry player tapped it into an empty net. It was a disaster to lose a nine-point lead, but that defeat was the makings of us in that we learned a valuable lesson. For years afterwards Nemo always played to the final whistle with no let-up.

The Nemo lads couldn't have been fairer to me. We went back to the Tory Top bar after the game and no one had a go. I think they all knew where my heart was.

I flew back to Strawberry Hill the next day with Frank Cogan's brother Billy, who was also on the course. I was a chastened man.

* * *

I was picked to go on the first All-Stars' tour to San Francisco, just a couple of weeks before I got married in 1971.

The All-Stars were picked from the seven counties with the most emigrants living in the San Francisco area. We went to Chicago first and then to San Francisco. I stayed with Mike Murphy in Chicago. The players stayed with the local Irish community on that trip and we couldn't have been looked after any better.

I got to play with Seán O'Neill of Down against Kerry, who were the All-Ireland champions. John Morley was there from Mayo and poor John was murdered while on Garda duty a few years later. It was my first time in The States and I stayed in Dan Culloty's house while we were in San Francisco. It was a home away from home and Dan's young son Danny would go on to win an All-Ireland with Cork when I was manager.

I married Mary on the 15th of April, 1971 in the Honan Chapel in UCC and the reception was held in Acton's Hotel in Kinsale. The Cork players gave us a guard of honour as we came out of the church and a great day was had by all.

We went back to Strawberry Hill and rented a flat in Teddington near the college. Mary got a job in a hotel in Richmond and we settled into married life. I was delighted Mary was with me in London even though I had been over and back quite a bit up to that for Cork games. Mary always backed me up in whatever I did.

I loved the course in Strawberry Hill. The exams went well. At last I was doing something I really loved and the study came easy.

It was back home to Cork for the summer.

Denis Coughlan had been sensationally dropped for the Kerry game in the Munster final and there was uproar. We had some fanatical supporters and they got a petition going to restore Denis to the team.

We were really upset about the dropping of Denis and there was talk that we might not play. In the end, we decided to tog out as we felt it might be going a bit too far.

Kerry got off to a great start, but the game changed when Denis came on after only ten minutes. He played a blinder. We won by 0-25 to 0-14 and Denis must have kicked about 11 points. I particularly remember Kevin Jer O'Sullivan's display. He was outstanding.

Offaly beat us in the All-Ireland semi-final. It was a fine Offaly team and they went on to win the All-Ireland again the following year. Once again, we failed to capitalise on beating Kerry.

Nemo won the Cork Intermediate hurling championship and I was playing right half-forward. We drew with Carrigtwohill who scored eight goals and a point against us in the first match.

The throw-in for the replay was delayed and some local character was asked why it was held up and the answer was 'Carrigtwohill are refusing to start before the Nemo 'keeper arrives.' We won the replay and it was a huge thing for the club.

My brother Noel played that day and he was a very good hurler. He was outstanding for us. We now had a senior hurling and football team. It was all the same players and I am convinced that if we had stuck purely with the hurling, we would have won a Cork Senior championship.

* * *

There was a lot of animosity in Kerry towards us after the marking of Mick O'Dwyer in the 1971 Munster final and there was a nasty atmosphere when we met Kerry in the league that November in Tralee. There was a needle from the very start in that game.

There was a lad in the crowd in his early twenties or late teens giving me a hard time. He posted himself at the back of the net and was dishing out abuse. He even kicked me through the net on a couple of occasions. Then this high ball came in and I thought it was going wide. I followed it round the back of the goals and started fighting with the young lad. I must have been fairly distracted because the ball actually hit the post and was cleared by a Cork defender. Eventually we separated when the ball was gone well up the field, but only after a few digs were thrown.

That was the day I really got to know Humphrey Kelleher. I think he always took a bit of pride in protecting me.

I was walking off the pitch with Humphrey when the game was over and a group of Kerry supporters were slagging us. A Cork fan ran by Humphrey, tapped him on the shoulder and shouted 'well done, Humphrey boy', but Humphrey thought he was being attacked by a Kerry supporter and he turned round with his fists in the air. Humphrey roared out 'come on, come on' to the Kerry crowd who were slagging us. They backed off.

We got into the dressing room. Humphrey threw off his jersey and he was some size of a man with a big hairy chest. Murty O'Shea, another huge man, was also in the dressing room. There was a few of the Kerry crowd still banging loudly on the dressing room door.

'Open the f\*\*king door,' shouted Humphrey and someone opened it.

The sight of two giants was enough to scatter the mob.

# CHAPTER 9

# *A County At Last*

PLAYERS ALWAYS LIKE TO HAVE A SAY IN WHO IS RUNNING THEIR TEAM. IT'S PERFECTLY understandable. With so much effort being put in, it's vital the man in charge has the support of everyone.

We were no different in Cork and the players approached Donie Donovan to become Cork coach early in 1972.

Donie told us he wanted to oversee all the coaching and physical training. From the start, he was his usual self and we were a happy squad. There was organisation and at the same time sympathy towards the players. We fancied ourselves, as you always had to, against Kerry.

The Munster final was held in Killarney on a very hot day against an ageing Kerry team. We were expected to run Kerry off the pitch as we had a young fit squad with players coming through from underage level.

The fact that it was also the first 80-minute Munster final seemed to be very much in our favour. Kerry led by two points at half-time and we fancied ourselves to outstay them in the second half.

I remember distinctly coming out to the goal at the dressing room end and Donie Sheahan, a Killarney chemist, went behind the goal and being a typical Kerry rogue he said, 'Billy, ye have us. Ye will run us off the pitch'.

It was a good insight into the Kerry psyche. I mean this in the best possible way, but that was their method of building you up – by knocking their own team when they were actually confident of winning. They've been at it ever since I can remember.

'Ah, I dunno Donie,' I said in reply but what with the heat and the age of the Kerry team, I agreed with him even though I didn't say as much.

Kerry got two goals at the start of the second half and try as we might we just could not pull them back. Conned yet again by Kerry.

I was to share a dressing room with the Kerry lads that year.

Munster hadn't won the Railway Cup for years and we were determined to win it back.

The Railway Cup was a very prestigious competition in those days. It was regarded as a great honour to be picked for your province as it meant you were considered by the selectors to be the best player in your position in the six counties of Munster. It's such a pity that the competition has slipped so far down the GAA rankings nowadays.

Babs Keating, Ray Cummins and Mick O'Dwyer made up the Munster full-forward line that day. Frank Cogan was midfield with Mick O'Connell and it was such a pleasure to play with O'Connell. There was great camaraderie within the team and it was a huge thrill to play with such legends. Munster won the Railway Cup after a replay.

\* \* \*

I was made captain and trainer/coach of Nemo later on that year.

I had a load of new ideas I brought back from Strawberry Hill. I designed specific drills and even the way we played was an attacking/possession type of football. It was something I had been thinking about for years and now that I had the run of the team, I was able to bring forward my own ideas.

I had no problem with getting the lads to play the way I wanted. We had won the minor double two years previously and we had six players on the field who played in that hugely significant win for the club. Kieran Collins and Liam Good were still minor. Seamus Coughlan was 19. Dinny Allen, John Corcoran, Dinna Driscoll, Colm Murphy and Brian Murphy were only 20.

I wasn't a selector and I had Dinny McDonnell with me who was totally on my side. He gave me a free hand in training the team. We had rows and we had it hot and heavy from time to time, but the way it was with Dinny was when it was over, it was over.

My vision of Gaelic football more or less saw it as a possession game that required a high degree of skill and fitness. I based the game on support play. Someone had to be in support of the player on the ball all the time. You could attack from the full-back line or the half-back line once the support was in place. The idea was to have an extra man all the time. If we were attacking, we would have the extra man and if the opposition team were attacking, the extra man would be back in defence. It was all about mobility, up and down the pitch.

* * *

We still didn't have our own grounds at Nemo and we played on a corporation pitch on the Tramore Road.

If you were in goal at the bottom end, you could only barely see the crossbar at the top end.

The dressing rooms were old railway carriages, but they got burned out and we togged out in cars, or if it was dry on the side of the pitch. Dinny Mac got some sort of dynamo and lights for training for the county final, but you could only see up to waist high.

We were very, very lucky to get a draw out of St Michael's Blackrock in the 1972 semi-final. Dinny Allen got a point in the last minute to equalise it for us.

In the replay, Michael's were playing with a strong breeze and were winning by 1-8 to 0-0. Jimmy Barrett got a goal just before half-time and it was that score that won it for us. It gave us hope going in and in the second half we came out and we won by 4-6 to 1-10. My brother Noel scored two goals – he was outstanding for us that day.

I was younger than Noel and I was his boss. He was nicknamed The Ghost in Nemo as he used to ghost in for goals. He didn't start in the drawn game and coming home after the last training session, I told him how disappointed I was for him. He just shrugged his shoulders and said 'that's the way it is'. And he never so much as said a word of complaint.

We met UCC in the final.

We were six up against wind and rain in the second half but we played typical Nemo tactics and kept the ball. Our plan was not to kick the ball away aimlessly and we operated on the assumption if we had the ball, they didn't. We weren't a big team and that type of game suited us. We were totally as one. Every one of us had gone to Críost Rí, bar Brother Fabien, and he taught there.

Frank Halbert was refereeing and we were well ahead when Moss Keane asked him if there was much time left.

'Three minutes, Moss,' replied Frank.

'Ah, for f\*\*k sake, Frank,' said Moss, 'blow the thing up and we'll go away for a few pints.'

The day after the match we met the College lads in The Star and from there we went down to Kinsale to Murphy's Hotel and all my college friends came with us. I remember Dinny Allen was up on Moss Keane's shoulders and was bouncing off lamps and everything else.

We were a small club at the time and it was a massive achievement.

Life was good. Nemo got to the senior county semi-final in hurling. I started teaching in Sully's Quay when I came home from Strawberry Hill and I took over the school's football team. We made it to the semi of the Frewen against Brendan's of Killarney and they had two great players who I would cross paths with again many times: Páidí ó Sé and a small little blondy fella called Pat Spillane.

I was very enthusiastic. I was in my dream job and it wasn't all PE. I was also teaching Irish and Geography, but PE was my first love. I was getting on very well with the teachers and especially the pupils. Peadar Garvan was vice-principal and he was a Nemo man. He couldn't have been more supportive.

I was playing football and training Nemo, playing hurling for Nemo, playing for Cork and training Sully's Quay.

Mary was brilliant. She came from a GAA family of ten girls. Her father Tommy Allen was a founder member of Kilbrittain GAA club and he brought the Allen girls to matches every Sunday. Mary loved the game and came along to most of my matches.

Mary was working in the Victoria Hotel in Cork city in a management job. The teacher's salary wasn't great at that time. There were no Spanish holidays or cruises for us, but we got by fine and our social life was a few drinks after a match on a Sunday night.

Our house cost £5,200 back in 1972 and of course we had a mortgage. When I think back, the £5,200 seemed enormous and I remember saying 'how are we ever going to manage to pay back the mortgage'.

Noel was still living at home with my dad in Tonyville when we moved into our own house. Noel completed his Masters and went off to Canada with Tony. My sister Mary went back to college and when she qualified she moved to Tipperary to take up a job as a teacher in Nenagh.

# CHAPTER 10

# *Sam On The Mantelpiece*

**NEMO'S COUNTY TITLE WAS A DREAM COME TRUE – IN MORE WAYS THAN ONE. THE CLUB** nominated me as captain of the Cork team for the year 1973. And there was an added bonus in that Dinny McDonnell became chairman of the Cork selectors.

The rule in Cork was the county champions had the right to appoint their own selector. Dinny was the ideal man for the job.

He was young and dynamic. We knew Dinny would do everything he possibly could to bring an All-Ireland back to Cork. He had all the qualities needed for the job. Dinny was very strong and he wasn't afraid to take on county players, myself included.

I remember one time when Nemo were playing a challenge match against Muskerry out in Kilmurray, only a fortnight before the 1970 Munster final against Kerry.

Frank Cogan and myself didn't want to play because we felt the challenge game was too close to the Munster final and we were afraid of picking up an injury. Dinny was club chairman and he put his foot down. He insisted we play.

'I'll put Nemo football up on a pedestal first,' he said to us, 'and if I do that, I will put Cork football up on pedestal.'

Dinny was also a Nemo selector and the driving force behind the club. He was the architect of the modern Nemo. We had great respect for Dinny and we did as he asked. We played the challenge match, even though we weren't too happy about it at the time.

Nemo had become very, very well organised and professional; a lot of that development was down to Dinny. He was very forceful and got things done.

When Dinny Mac, as we called him, got involved with Cork, he immediately began to put structures in place.

Dinny gave his full backing to Donie Donovan as team trainer and that was a move that made us players very happy.

It was the players who approached Donie to train the team the previous year. Dinny knew the trainer would need our full backing. Dinny's first move was to make sure Donie would get his way when it came to picking the team.

This might be seen as the norm today, but back in '73 the team trainer was not a selector and indeed this was the case for a good few years after that.

Dinny made sure he sat next to Donie at our games, and if Donie wanted to make changes, he did his best to get what Donie wanted. Dinny being Dinny, he succeeded in having Donie's changes accepted nearly all of the time. He was a pragmatist and he knew Donie should be the main man.

Dinny had no ego and all he wanted was the best for the team.

He set about putting a back-up team in place. Donie brought in my old UCC mentor, Dr Paddy Fitzgerald. John 'Kid' Cronin, who was an ex-boxer living out in Blackpool, in the heart of the Glen, came in as masseur. He was also a great character. You need to have characters around a team.

The Kid stayed with us for years. It was the last few seconds before we went out for the 1988 All-Ireland final against Meath. We were fisting the ball around in a circle and I kept at the players to concentrate. The Kid was in the circle and he dropped the ball. He was in his seventies at the time. I was well up for the game. 'Kid,' I shouted, 'for f**k sake, will you concentrate'. No one laughed. That was The Kid. He was especially kind to young players who came into the squad. He'd sit beside them almost unnoticed and chat to them, putting them at their ease. He was always telling jokes and 'the dropped ball' was one of his favourites.

For the first time in a long time, we had organisation and structure in Cork. And from an early stage in '73 you felt something could happen.

Nevertheless, our results in the 1972-73 National League were indifferent and we failed to make the closing stages.

The selectors had tried out a lot of new players and that worked out in that by the end of the league we had a fairly settled team. Cork always had problems in taking their chances and we found two new forwards.

Billy Field came in and Jimmy Barry Murphy played in the last match of the league against Longford.

JBM, as we called him, did well against Longford. There was nothing much at stake, but he showed for the ball all the time. It was the little darts he made and the little quick, skilful touches that made him special.

We were getting on well together. There was a fierce spirit within the camp and to this day we are all great friends.

We played a challenge down the 'Dyke against the Defence Forces a week or two before the Munster final and JBM showed up very well at full-forward against Jack Cosgrove of Galway, who was the All-Star full-back the previous year. JBM was only 18 at the time and it would have been seen as a big gamble to play him at full-forward in a Munster final. He used to arrive into the dressing room with a skinhead haircut and wore all the gear – the short denims above the ankles, the denim jacket and wide braces, the Doc Martins, the lot.

Some of the older County Board men couldn't make head nor tail out of it all and that gave the players no end of pleasure. The common view was that skinheads were violent thugs, but JBM was exactly the opposite of that. He was totally unassuming – a lovely fella. JBM was just following the fashion and wearing the same gear as his friends.

His dress may not have been traditional, but he came from a solid GAA background. His granduncle Dinny Barry Murphy won several All-Ireland hurling medals for Cork.

Kerry were the hottest favourites for years, but we fancied our chances even though we were a bit disappointed when it was raining on the morning of the match. In previous years, the rain might have suited Cork as it would have evened things up, but not now. The team was full of skilful footballers and the dry ball would have suited us.

Thank God, the weather did clear up and there was the most incredible opening in all the history between Kerry and Cork.

We went five goals up! The score after 23 minutes was 5-3 to 0-3. Kerry didn't know what hit them.

Donie outsmarted Kerry. He moved Ray Cummins, who was picked at full-forward, out to the corner. Paudie O'Donoghue, the Kerry full-back had no choice but to follow him out. There was loads of space in front of goal and we played quick ball into JBM, who was brilliant. We ripped Kerry apart.

Cummins kicked four points and JBM trapped a ball that came off the upright even though Jimmy Deenihan was bearing down on him. It just showed how skilful and cool he was. JBM slotted it home, soccer-style, with his left.

I made a couple of fairly good saves from Mickey Ned O'Sullivan and Mick O'Dwyer early on in the game. Funnily enough, I was to coach Cork against the two Kerrymen in the years that followed.

Kerry fought back and in the second half we were only five points up when Kerry's Jackie Walsh took a fierce shot. I just managed the save. It was one of those special days.

The field was a sea of red after the game. It took us ages to get to the dressing rooms. As captain, I was lifted off my feet onto someone's shoulders. I couldn't stop them and I was a small bit embarrassed.

I knew we still had two games to go to win the All-Ireland.

We went to Paddy Crowley's in Oliver Plunkett Street for a few pints after the game. The talk was of the five goals, but we reminded ourselves that we had beaten Kerry by 11 points two years previously and had failed to finish the job.

Unbelievably, we also scored five goals in the semi-final against Tyrone. Seamus Coughlan came on and scored 1-1. That showed the strength of our panel and it stood to us all the year. Even though we scored five goals, we didn't play well. The game had no shape to it. Tyrone ran and ran, but there was no method to their game. The newspapers were very hard on Tyrone and they weren't too gone on us either, which did us no harm at all in the build-up for the final against Galway.

Galway were made firm favourites but at the time I remember saying to someone that 'we didn't give a f**k who were favourites'. That was the way we felt. Everything was done for us. The attention to detail was inspiring.

There was a toss before the final to decide which team would hold on to their colours as there was a clash between our red jerseys and Galway's maroon strip.

Galway won the toss and we had to find an all-white jersey with red cuffs. Tyrone, in fairness to them, sent down their jerseys and we trained in the same colours we were going to be wearing in the All-Ireland final.

That got us used to picking out players when we were under pressure; a split second can make all the difference in an All-Ireland.

It came down to that in terms of our thinking and preparation. The smallest little detail was looked after. We went up to Dublin by train on the day before the game and we stayed in the Skylon Hotel, just up the road from Croke Park.

I always get keyed up before big matches, but I used an old Cork cure to get myself to sleep the night before the game.

I used to go off the drink for about three weeks before every championship game. I was very nervous on the night before my first All-Ireland semi-final against Galway in 1966 and I couldn't sleep. I got out of bed, put on my clothes and went for a walk around.

Weesh Murphy, the chairman, and Eamonn Young were having a drink in the hotel bar. Weesh was always on the look-out for me and he asked what was up. I told him I couldn't get to sleep.

'Do ya drink?' he asked me.

'I do,' I said, in a slightly apologetic voice.

Then Youngy asked, 'What do you drink?'

'A pint of Guinness.'

Weesh ordered and paid for a pint.

I sipped away and chatted with the Weesh and Youngy.

Weesh ordered a second pint of Guinness and I drank that one, as instructed.

'Now young fella,' said Youngy, 'go on away up to bed.'

Of course that method of getting players to relax wouldn't be contemplated now, but I fell off to sleep the minute my head hit the pillow.

I was just as nervous the night before the 1973 final.

We were a very united bunch and we went to the Ivy House pub, just across the road from the Skylon.

We drank two pints a man. There was a table full of empty glasses by the time we got to the end of second pint, as you can well imagine with 20 or so of us drinking two pints each.

We drank two pints on the night before the semi-final in the very same pub, but there was very few around then.

The Ivy House is very close to Croke Park and the pub was packed with Cork supporters who were staying in the area. We weren't expecting that.

A shocked supporter came over to our table.

'All the drink ye're havin' and ye're playin' in the All-Ireland final tomorrow. And ye are all pissed.' He walked away shaking his head – disgusted with our carry-on. You can imagine the rumours that started up over that one! The two pints did the trick yet again, though, and I slept well.

JBM's pals were up to support him and they had no room for the night. Dinny McDonnell gave JBM permission to put them up in his room on one condition: JBM got the bed.

Donie was nice and calm on Sunday morning and that helped us to stay calm.

There was a team meeting on the morning of the match. Frank and myself were a minute late. Dinny laid into us. That was his way. He had no favourites. The fact we were very friendly with Dinny and came from Nemo made no difference to him.

I said a few words about Weesh Murphy at the team meeting. Weesh died outside the Skylon Hotel just three weeks before the final. Dr Con, his son, was and is one of my best friends.

I was very moved when Weesh's wife sent up the scapular Weesh wore in the 1945 final.

The scapular was a long brown cord with a picture of the Sacred Heart attached at the end. You wore it around your neck and I wore Weesh's scapular in the final.

The late Dermot O'Brien, who captained Louth to beat Cork in 1957, asked permission to address us in the dressing room. Donie okayed it and Dermot wished us luck. Dinny Mac had a rule though that there was to be only voice in the dressing room and that was Donie's.

Donie didn't get too worked up at the team meeting. He was quietly spoken and it worked. We felt calm and reassured. There was a fierce air of confidence about us.

There was no shouting or roaring in the dressing room. There was no need. We were totally focused.

Galway got off to a great start. Nineteen-year-old Morgan Hughes scored a great free from over 40 yards out. He caused a lot of bother early on, but Frank Cogan got to grips with him and shut him out after that.

Dinny Long took a free from about 40 yards out and it hit the upright. Jimmy Barrett fisted down the rebound and JBM palmed it into the back of the net. There were only two minutes gone and it settled us. We went in six points up.

Donie was very reassuring at half-time. It wasn't so much what he said, but the way he said it. Our attitude was 'we're only half-way there'.

Early in the second half, Tommy Naughton took a shot. I dived to my right. I got a hand to it. The ball hit the post and rebounded back off me. I turned back and the ball definitely wasn't over the line. The umpire waved the green flag. Little did I know that that goal would have repercussions in a Munster final three years later. That brought Galway to within four points. We held our lead and then JBM struck. I'll never forget the exact moment he scored that goal right at the end.

I dropped to my knees and said, 'Bill, that's it now. You've won your All-Ireland medal'.

It was a feeling of absolute euphoria. All my life I wanted an All-Ireland medal and I had it now. Galway scored a consolation goal immediately afterwards with just seconds left and the poacher Jimmy Barrett got one back for us with the last kick of the game.

We won by seven points. The Cork supporters climbed over the wire on to the pitch and they were waiting behind my goal for the final whistle. Johnny Bowen was the first out on the pitch. Johnny was on the school team in Sully's Quay and it meant so much to me that one of my pupils was the first out to congratulate me. I was overjoyed.

There was pandemonium and it took ages to get through the crowd and go up to collect the Sam Maguire Cup.

I didn't prepare my speech as I thought it would be unlucky. I was teaching Irish at the time and my Irish was good enough so I had no fears when it came to that part of it. Strangely, I wasn't nervous. I told the crowd we won it for Weesh.

Then, totally off the cuff, I congratulated Tyrone for winning the minor All-Ireland and said 'we down here don't do enough for the people up North'. That was of course during the terrible days of the Troubles when GAA people were targeted not only by the UVF but also by the security forces. Players were stopped on the way to training and arrested just because they were members of the GAA.

I met a fella later that year and he asked me if I was Billy Morgan? 'I am,' I said. He had a strong northern accent. 'Did you mean what you said up on that stand?' I told him I meant every word of it.

'Put it there,' he said and he offered me his hand. That small gesture of support was very well received up north even though there were some who maintained I shouldn't have brought politics into sport. I would do the same again if I got the chance. We in the south never fully appreciated what the GAA were going through in the north. I was tipped off through a friend that the Special Branch had been watching me after the All-Ireland speech. At the time, the Special Branch were charged with keeping an eye on the IRA, but I had nothing to do with the IRA. All I wanted to do was show a bit of solidarity with the GAA in the north of Ireland.

We went to the Ivy House on the way back to the Skylon for the first pint. And that first pint after winning your first All-Ireland is the sweetest you will ever drink. There was a reception that night and we were given two tickets each for the banquet in the Green Isle Hotel. Mary's sister Imelda was home from America and I gave her one of my tickets and of course Mary got the other. Connie Hartnett, who played a blinder at wing-back, did something similar with his ticket.

We thought we would have no bother getting in. We had the base of the cup with us. Someone else had brought the actual cup in.

We were asked for our tickets at the door by the security man. By now, Dinny Mac had arrived and so had several of the players. They wouldn't let Connie and myself in. The players wouldn't go in without us. That was the way with us; we always stuck together. Some of the players were already inside at this stage. Dinny Mac said, 'If Billy and Connie can't go in, none of us are going in.'

Con Murphy the honorary secretary and Frank Murphy, who was an employee of the Cork County Board, were called out. Con said, 'If ye don't have tickets, ye can't get in.' There was a good few players still waiting outside.

Eventually, they let us, but I was seething when I saw all the politicians sitting down eating. Although I must say the Lord Mayor at the time Pat Kerrigan was as nice a man as you could meet. I hate those banquets anyway. I was seated at the top table and I was the only member of the team sitting there.

I had a few words to say to the guests.

'How is it that I'm the only player up here at the top table? And why isn't Donie Donovan up here?' I left it at that.

I couldn't wait to get out of there.

My abiding memory of the next day was of the journey on a lorry through my native city with half of Cork hanging off it. Someone put a garland of a laurel leaf around my neck and we travelled out of the railway station and up the Lower Road and MacCurtin Street. Then there was the turn round Barry's Corner. You're looking down Patrick Street at thousands of people. It was just a red sea all the way. Forget about Moses looking down on the Holy Land – the view from the All-Ireland winning lorry as you round Barry's Corner is the greatest sight a Corkman could ever see.

# CHAPTER 11

# *'You'll Never See A Nemo Man On His Own'*

THE GOOD DAYS JUST KEPT ON COMING. THE SECOND BIG BONUS FROM NEMO'S COUNTY TITLE win was that we were in the All-Ireland club championship for the first time.

We won the Munster Club title when we beat Kenmare of Kerry and Doonbeg of Clare.

Fr Griffin's from Galway were our opponents in the All-Ireland semi-final. The Nemo squad went up to Ennis the night before and stayed in the West County Hotel. It was great for the lads and a whole new experience for most of Nemo. We hammered Fr Griffin's by 0-17 to 0-9. Jimmy Barrett was absolutely superb. He kicked points from all angles in one of Nemo's greatest days. I was still player/coach and here I was in an All-Ireland club final in only my second year in the job.

The final was against St Vincent's of Dublin in Portlaoise. This was the very club Nemo and Dinny McDonnell wanted to use as a template. Vincent's built the team on a strong local presence and like us most of the players had been either at school together, or had played underage for the club.

We were leading by a point with minutes to go and Seamus Coughlan went through the middle and hammered a shot off the crossbar. He hit it so hard it bounced back about 30 yards out the field. Vincent's regained possession and were awarded a free about 60 yards out. Jimmy Keaveney put it straight over the bar.

We always had a facility for getting goals and we scored four against Vincent's in the replay.

Dinny Allen was playing soccer with Hibs and Nemo had a rule that it was one or the other. The rule had nothing to do with the GAA ban and had to do with the commitment Nemo needed. We all accepted the rule. Dinny was still very much one of us and went to all the matches, but it just gives you an idea of how determined you have to be to get to the top.

There was a mentality in Nemo that we were still the new kids on the block and we were never the elite. We are often accused of being clannish and in a way we are. Most of us went to school together. First it was Sully's Quay in the fifties and later Scoil Chríost Rí and then Coláiste Chríost Rí.

We were all very good friends. It's nearly like a war cry now, but it was Frank Cogan who summed it up best when he said: 'You'll never see a Nemo man on his own'. There will always be four or five of us together.

Eddie Brophy from Number 5 in Tonyville was full-back in those Nemo teams. We grew up together and had been friends since we were kids and learned our sport on The Pitch or up against the Red Gate on Higha. That was significant for me and it really sums up what we were about. Eddie captained Nemo when we won the intermediate hurling title and it was a special day for the club without a home. And Eddie's young lad Paul is playing for Nemo now.

So that was it, we were All-Ireland club champions. I always wanted to get the most out of every team. The funny thing was that by the time we were club champions, we had been knocked out of the Cork County Championship by the 'Barrs in the first round, but no one can ever take that All-Ireland club away from us.

\* \* \*

This was my second year training the Sully's Quay team and we beat, of all teams, Coláiste Chríost Rí in the Frewen Cup Munster Under-17 final. I had mixed feelings about that, but I had a job to do and I did it.

I could put all of my own ideas into that team and I really loved it. It was a great place to try out new moves and I got on extremely well with the lads who went along with me 100 per cent. Gene Desmond was captain of that team, and I later played behind him in a Munster final.

I was as happy as ever in the school and I must say I loved my job.

I won the Texaco Player of the Year award in 1973 and I was sole nomination for goalkeeper in the All-Star team. More bonuses. But most important of all was that I was now an All-Ireland medal winner. It was all I ever dreamed of.

\* \* \*

And I was in demand.

The GAA ban had been lifted in 1971 and Waterford asked me to sign as cover for League of Ireland legend, Peter Thomas.

I heard nothing much from Waterford until October when another friend Jackie Morley, who was involved with Waterford, asked me if I wanted to play in the League Cup final against Finn Harps in Tolka Park. Peter Thomas was injured so I was on the spot. I was in no shape to play anything after three weeks on the rip since winning the All-Ireland.

I didn't want to make an eejit out of myself. And there's a big difference between playing in goal in football and soccer. I really wanted to play at least one game at that level. I only made up my mind to play on the morning of the match.

I got the last class off from the boss in Sully's Quay and I was to meet a taxi driver called Tony who used to drive the Cork players. I met up with Tony in Patrick Street and the traffic was horrendous.

By the time we got to Watergrasshill, just outside the city, we lost about an hour. I asked Tony if we'd make it but he said we wouldn't. I rang Shay Brennan, the former Manchester United star and then the Waterford manager, and told him as much. He didn't say too much and it all worked out fine as Waterford won 2-1.

There was a skit on television the following Sunday night that highlighted me stuck in a traffic jam in Watergrasshill and there was a cartoon of me in the taxi surrounded by cattle and sheep. Nothing could be further from the truth. I was in the news a fair bit at the time having just captained Cork to win the All-Ireland and it made a good story even if the feckin' traffic jam was in Patrick Street!

# CHAPTER 12

# The Dubs Ambush Us

**THIS WAS THE YEAR OF THE DUBS.**

I was very friendly with the Dublin full-forward Jimmy Keaveney, and I still am. We invited Jimmy and his wife Angela, who was very close to Mary, down to Cork for the August weekend in 1974.

Frank Cogan married Mary's twin sister Anne and they asked the Keaveneys over to their house for lunch on the Bank Holiday Monday. The Sam Maguire cup happened to be in Frank's house at the time and as Jimmy was walking out the path to his car, Frank and myself went back in and grabbed the Sam.

'Jimmy, Jimmy,' I called out, and Jimmy turned around.

'Take a good luck at the cup, Jim. It's the nearest ye'll come to it.'

Big mistake. And what did Jimmy do? He went back to Dublin and told the Dublin manager Kevin Heffernan what had happened and Kevin used it afterwards in the dressing room before our semi-final against the Dubs. And how Keaveney enjoys telling that one, even after all these years.

Cork were a confident team in 1974, and there was a special bond between the players. We had an indifferent league campaign, but we weren't overly worried about that after our successes the previous year.

Donie warned us that we should put a stop to the celebrations after Christmas. There was a celebratory event staged somewhere in Cork nearly every night of the week.

We were treated like gods, particularly in the football areas like West Cork and Millstreet, and you could be out morning, noon and night if you wanted to. I was expected to attend a whole range of functions as captain and while I enjoyed every minute of it, we probably overdid the celebrations.

That year's Munster final was against Kerry in Killarney. Kerry were in a period of transition. Mick O'Dwyer retired for good this time and youngsters such as Ger Power, Páidí Ó Sé and Mikey Sheehy were brought in. We were full of confidence.

There was a good few of us having a few pints in the Imperial Hotel one night after training, about two weeks before we were due to play Kerry.

'Are you lot the Cork football team?' asked this commercial traveller from Roscommon. We told him we were.

'Ah,' he said, ' and here ye are boozing while Kerry are in bed.'

'But are they sleeping?' asked Jimmy Barrett.

The day of the final was horrible and wet. Kerry had the wind and rain in the first half and Humphrey Kelleher and myself had particularly good games. Kerry went in only two points up at half-time.

It was Mick O'Connell's last game. Frank Cogan and myself joked with Dinny Long that it would be nice to see him doing to Micko what Micko did to him a few years previously. O'Connell sold Dinny a few dummies and play-acted a bit with the ball in front of Dinny.

And it came to pass. It was late in the game and Dinny started to bounce the ball in front of Micko and the Kerry crowd didn't like it very much. Micko had to give in to age and the effects of an inter-county career that lasted nearly 20 years.

We hammered Kerry that day and in a way it was the worst thing that could have happened to us.

Dublin were our opponents in the semi-final. It was the start of a GAA revolution that would change the game forever. The Dubs had been promoted from Division 2 and while they were an improving team, they were given no chance against us.

Brian, our first child, was born on the 30th July that year, 11 days before the semi-final and the whole team celebrated after training that night.

Brian's birth was one of the greatest moments of our lives. There was no going in to attend the birth or anything like that in those days and I suppose it beats any All-Ireland win when you see one of your kids for the first time.

We didn't realise that Kevin Heffernan had brought the fitness of his players to new levels. Cork kind of felt Dublin had come out of the second division, won a Leinster and would be satisfied with that. They said as much in the build-up and we believed them.

We could hear the soccer-like chants before the game in the dressing rooms under the stands. Even though we were seasoned campaigners, we never heard anything like it. The singing and the chanting and the clapping went through the walls. When we came out on to the pitch, the atmosphere was like nothing we had experienced before. Dublin colonised The Hill and were the first group of supporters to wear the team jersey. There were banners, songs and chants to rival anything you would see in English soccer.

We felt if we got on top early on and picked off a few scores, Dublin would cave in. It was an ambush. Dublin went at us from the start and led all through. We were four points down with about ten minutes to go. I looked up at the scoreboard and I said to myself, 'if we're not careful here, we might be beaten'.

I still didn't realise, even that late in the game, that we were up against a really good, well-trained team. We were beaten by four points in the end. Dublin ran us off the pitch. Donie's warnings came true and we lost our title.

Dublin, of course, went on to win the All-Ireland.

\* \* \*

We had Brian now and we took every second turn to get up to feed him. He certainly took our minds off football for all the right reasons, but there was always Nemo and we again went to the county final against Carbery. They were a very good team, but we beat them by a goal. I was still player/coach and that win gave us enormous satisfaction, mainly due to the quality of the opposition. Back then we were very popular among the Cork footballing public. It was only a few years now since we made the breakthrough and we were still flying the flag for the smaller clubs.

By now, we had moved to our new pitches on the Back Douglas Road with proper dressing rooms and a bar. Again Dinny Mac spearheaded the move but the whole club got behind him and we thought we were the bee's knees. Nemo, after all the years, finally had a home.

That was also the year we brought off one of the biggest shocks in the history of Cork hurling when we beat the Glen in the first round of the Cork Senior championship. It was huge at the time. I played right half-forward and moved to midfield later on in what was one of my better days. The Glen had big names such as Denis Coughlan, Teddy O'Brien, Martin and Pat O'Doherty and Jerry O'Sullivan.

We met Blackrock in the semi and at the time they were county and All-Ireland champions. We were leading by a point with two minutes to go, but the Rockies came back and beat us by two points. I was playing midfield with Jimmy Barrett against 17-year-old Tom Cashman and Frank Cummins of Kilkenny, who was a superstar. Cashman was hardly known outside the Rockies back in those days. Georgie Allen, our coach, came to Jimmy Barrett and myself in the dressing room before the game and asked who should mark Frank Cummins. I kept my mouth shut. I definitely didn't want to mark Cummins. 'I'll take him', said Jimmy. 'I don't mind at all.'

I was delighted to get off Cummins and felt I would destroy young Cashman. Tom didn't give me a puck of the ball. I was taken off, and rightly so. Tom Cashman went on to become one of the finest hurlers Cork ever produced.

I think Nemo had a good attitude where football and hurling were concerned. Whatever came up next, we took it on, whether it be football or hurling. It was the same lads who were involved and there was never any friction in the club, or any pressure to choose football over hurling.

Mary must have been under pressure back then. I was involved in some sort of sport nearly all the time, but she never said a word. In addition to Cork and Nemo, I was still training Sully's Quay. She kept everything going at home. Mary understood more than anyone that I was at my happiest when I was involved in sport and she made sure I was happy.

Sully's Quay reached the Munster Senior schools final and we were beaten by St Brendan's after going four points up with eight minutes to go. Harry Houdini, or Ger O'Sullivan, who was to be my selector in the last few years I spent managing Cork, was playing for Brendan's. He was captain and was involved in the three goals they scored to win the game. I still hadn't won that Munster colleges title and we were gutted.

Sully's Quay made a terrible start to the following season in 1975 and were beaten by 18 points in a challenge by Tralee CBS. But we made steady progress and reached the Munster Senior final against the same opposition. Their star player was Seán Walsh and a year later he would score a disputed goal against me in a Munster final. Theo Cullinane did a good job in marking Seán that day. Dermot McCurtin was on that team and he went on to become an outstanding hurler for Cork.

Tralee missed a penalty and we won it by a point. It was to be a great year for the school. Georgie Allen coached the hurlers to win the Harty Cup. We were beaten in the All-Ireland semi after a replay.

They were a great bunch of lads. I had enormous respect for every one of them and every now and then we meet up to celebrate that famous win for the school.

\* \* \*

I felt this might be one of those special years. We had won the Munster colleges and now I focused on the county.

Cork were beaten by a very young Kerry team in the 1974-75 League, but we didn't take much notice. We were hot favourites to beat Kerry in the Munster final.

Dinny Allen was back from Cork Hibs and we started like we were going to annihilate Kerry. Dinny was on young Páidí ó Sé and he gave him a tough time early on, kicking over two quick points.

We then missed two kickable frees and from the kickouts Kerry came up the field. Brendan Lynch, my UCC pal, kicked a fine point and then Kerry got another to equalise.

Then disaster struck. A speculative kick came in towards our goal. I was at the post and it was lobbing into my chest. From nowhere one of our backs came and deflected it past me and into the net.

Kerry's tails were up then and they ran us off the pitch. The rest is, of course, history and many of that Kerry team went on to win eight All-Ireland medals. But what would have happened if we scored those two early frees to go four points up? Kerry were under pressure at the time. You know what they're like in Kerry when things aren't going well. We were going for three-in-a-row against them. Mick O'Dwyer was their trainer and he changed the course of football history.

Donie was in no way to blame. He warned us we were in trouble, but through no fault of Donie's, some our players weren't fit enough.

We were very disappointed. I thought we had three or four All-Ireland titles in us. At the time I didn't think Kerry would go on to achieve what they did over the next decade or so.

I knew from the start Mikey Sheehy was a genius and John Egan likewise. Pat Spillane was only a small fella in the corner, but you could see he was going to mature into a special player. I honestly don't think they became a super team until The Bomber Liston came into the side in 1978 and I always felt we could put it up to them.

\* \* \*

There were compensations that year however.

Nemo won the county final and again reached the All-Ireland club final only to be beaten by UCD in a cracking game. Eugene McGee was their manager and they had a superb, well-coached team. We were two up with ten minutes to go and referee PJ McGrath gave, in my opinion, two soft frees to UCD. Years later I felt he did the same thing to Kerry in the five-in-a-row final of 1982 when he gave Offaly two soft frees to put them within striking distance of Kerry. UCD went on to beat us by two points in the end.

I stayed on in the Skylon Hotel with Jimmy Barry Murphy, who had won an All-Ireland club earlier that day with the 'Barrs in the hurling. Both the 'Barrs and Nemo travelled home together on the train, but we had to remain in Dublin to play for Munster in the Railway Cup.

JBM was celebrating his win and I was drowning my sorrows.

We went to the St Vincent's club dinner out in Clontarf. We had a mighty night and only got back to the Skylon at four in the morning.

I was dying with a hangover the next day. JBM was nearly worse. He only touched the ball five times in the entire match, but he scored four goals and I saved a penalty. We look like death warmed up, but we went on to win the Railway Cup that day.

We beat Dohenys in the 1975 county championship and then we were to meet Austin Stacks of Tralee in the 1976 Munster Club final.

This wasn't so much a game as a saga of three amazing football matches. Stacks had Ger Power, Mikey Sheehy, John O'Keeffe, Ger O'Keeffe, and Anthony O'Keeffe who were all on the Kerry squad. Jo Jo Barrett, the writer and former Kerry player who went on to train Stacks to win an All-Ireland, was their excellent full-forward. Cork's Dinny Long was playing midfield for the Tralee side, but we managed to beat them after three of the best games I was ever lucky enough to play in. I got a firm reminder, though, that I was pushing on.

I was soloing out with a ball and I sent a pass to Colm Murphy, but it was intercepted by Ger Power. I was about 30 yards out and Power went straight for goal at lightning speed. Frank Cogan and myself started to chase back, but we couldn't get near Power who was just flying. Frank and myself just looked at each other and smiled.

Here we were, getting a little bit older and slower trying to chase this flyer. We had no chance of catching him and we never would. Ger was pulled down and Mikey Sheehy slotted the penalty.Mikey never scored a penalty against me in inter-county football, but he never missed one against me in a club match.

We won that last game in the trilogy by the skin of our teeth. It could have gone eitherway and the game ebbed and flowed from end to end with absolutely no let-up.

Vincent's beat us well in the semi-final. Midfielders, Brian Mullins and Fran Ryder, who were only young lads at the time, wouldn't let

BILLY MORGAN: REBEL REBEL

the ball cross the half-way line. They were outstanding that day and years later they looked after me very well in New York, but that's another story. Keaveney stayed on that night as did Tony Hanahoe – another man I got to know well over the years and for whom I have the greatest admiration and respect.

I first came across Keaveney after he scored two goals in me back in 1967 when we met Dublin in a National League game, but there was no more than the usual handshake after the match. A few weeks later, I went up to Dublin to follow UCC in the Fitzgibbon Cup. We ended up in the Olympic Ballroom and who should I spot dancing with this good-looking girl only Keaveney. I was half-cut and approached him.

'Hey you. Come over here. You scored two goals on me two weeks ago.' The girl he was with disappeared as the slagging started between us. The girl's name was Angela and it was the first night he met her. He spent the rest of the night looking for the pretty girl, but to no avail.

Two weeks later, I was playing with Munster against Leinster in Croke Park. I spotted Jimmy on the bench for Leinster. I was all embarrassed. His girl deserted him because of my antics in the Olympic.

'Howya Billy,' greeted Keaveney. 'What ya doin' after the match? Are ya goin' for a pint?' It was typical Keaveney.

And we met for a pint. We've been friends ever since and as for Angela, well Keaveney did manage to meet up with her again. In fact, he married her. The Keaveneys and the Morgans are great friends. Jimmy and myself often go away for a few days. We are very close and the friendship came about because of Gaelic football.

I treasure All-Irelands, but the friendships mean more to me. And I have managed to stay friends with most of my opponents over the years.

I seem to have been able to distinguish between the relationship on the pitch and off the pitch without really thinking about it too much. It just happened. I'm just a different man on the field of play or on the sideline. The game takes over and that's it. There's no holding back. Sometimes people may have difficulty in separating the man on the pitch with the after-match man. It's hard to explain unless you've been there and I know there are times when I overstepped the mark, but that's me and that's just the way the game gets so much inside of me when I'm in the middle of the action.

Sometimes I put on the act just to get the boys going. My first Munster final in charge of Cork was in 1987 and Niall Cahalane was hounding Pat Spillane. Pat was on the ground after being fouled by Niall and the referee Pat Lane from Limerick was about to take action. To those looking on, it may well have seemed that I lost the head when I ran on to the pitch to have a go at Pat Lane, but I was in total control.

'He's bluffing all day,' I said.

Now Pat went to ground a bit too easily at times, but in fairness Niall was giving him a right pasting. I think I might have got to the ref a bit after that, but then there were other occasions when I genuinely lost the cool. That's just me and it's as if the football field is a different world to the one outside the wire.

And yes I am good friends with Spillane. Let no one take it away from him. He was one of the greatest footballers of all time. It's nice to be friends after matches, but during matches is a different scenario altogether. You use what you can.

# CHAPTER 13

# *Goodbye*

**BY NOW, MY FATHER WAS LIVING WITH US IN BISHOPSTOWN. MY FATHER USED TO GO TO MY** sister Mary in Nenagh around April every year. I said goodbye to him the morning he left and he wished me well in our next game against Derry.

I got a phone call from my brother-in-law Brian McDonnell in Nenagh. My father had dropped dead while digging the garden – it was a heart attack. He was 76.

I will never forget that precise moment. It was terrible shock as you might imagine.

There was some consolation in that when my aunt died a year earlier, also from a heart attack my father said to me, 'Billy, that's the way I'd like to go.'

We got on very well, especially in later years. I am glad he was around long enough to enjoy his retirement and take things easy. It can't have been easy trying to hold down a job and rear a family on your own. My son Brian was two when my dad died and he was his first grandchild. My father was mad about Brian and loved his company. He was one of those men who just loved kids.

As I said, I only really got to understand my dad when I was older and especially after I read his letter to Aunt Mary when my mother was sick.

It's only now that I have a family of my own that I realise the effort he had to put in to rearing us. He always put his family first.

It's not one of my traits to show affection openly, even though I do have the feelings inside of me for those I care about. Don't ask me why I can't open up more. Maybe that's where the anger comes from. That's just me.

And I ask myself why I didn't talk to him more. There was no hint he was going to die. If he had been sick, I could have said things to him. It was the suddenness of his death that got to me. You just get so caught up in work, your own family and the football that there seems to be no time to sit down and talk. The strange thing is there is plenty of time, but it just doesn't seem that way. I would have loved to have shown affection openly for Dad back then, but you can't turn back the clock.

My father was Galway to the last. He was buried in Killallaghton Cemetery beside my mother. He had always said he would go back to Galway when he retired, but he never got around to it.

\* \* \*

Life goes on and so does the All-Ireland championship. In a way, it was an escape and football will always take your mind off things.

The following year, 1976, saw some new faces emerge in the cork football set-up.

The County Board gave the nomination of selectors for the county team to Nemo. Dinny McDonnell opted out. He felt he had done his bit for Cork, but he left the team in good hands. Paddy Sullivan and Donal Barrett were the two Nemo men on the selection committee. Donie was finally appointed as a selector. Toots Kelleher from Millstreet was a former Cork star and Mick Farr out of the Dohenys was also an excellent choice.

The players will tell you straight away the minute a selection committee is named whether or not they will be any good. We were happy when we heard who was to be in charge.

It was the first year Dr Con Murphy was involved and my old college friend was not only an excellent doctor but a good friend to all the players. His door was always open and the word 'no' wasn't in his vocabulary. He was always pro-player unlike some who saw players as an obstacle in the efficient management of the bureaucracy.

The system in Cork was crazy in those days. Dinny Mac, who was such a huge part of our All-Ireland win in 1973, was no longer a selector in 1974 – just because Nemo didn't win the county the previous year. There was no continuity and some of the selectors just weren't up to the job with little or no experience of inter-county football.

* * *

Cork played Clare in the Championship in Thurles and we won comfortably. We went back to the Anner Hotel after the match. There was a big crowd there and I spotted two Clare lads who soldiered with me in Strawberry Hill. We had a chat and a drink and then later on in the evening I became isolated from the Cork lads and my Clare friends.

These two Clare supporters, whom I had never met before, came on over towards me. They were insulting and trying to belittle me. One word borrowed another and things got hot and heavy.

One of them pushed a glass in my face and the blood started to spurt out. 'Big Bird' from Nemo waded in and fair play to him, he put the two Clare lads away before they could do further damage. I threw a few punches and the two attackers weren't much use when it came to a fair fight.

I was brought into the toilet and I could see the state of my face in the mirror. There was an open gash and the blood was still spurting out – I have a horseshoe-shaped scar on my jaw to this day. I was stitched up that night in Thurles by a local doctor and I went home, without going to hospital.

I told Mary I was caught by a stud as I went down for the ball and as a GAA woman she accepted that as part of the game. Mary was well used to me coming home all battered and bruised, although since the rule was brought in that goalkeepers couldn't be shoulder-charged there weren't as many injuries. Up to then, it was open season with big full-forwards doing their best to drive you out through the back of the net. And never expect an unblemished face if you play hurling.

The following day a priest who was involved with Clare rang the house. Mary answered the phone and the priest asked how I was.

'He's fine,' said Mary. 'Sure, it was only an accident anyway.'

'It was no such thing,' said the priest, 'I'm ashamed to say Billy was glassed in the face.'

I came home from school and Mary told me about the phone call. She didn't give me a hard time and that was the end of it. Looking back on it now, we laugh at the whole affair, but I still have the scar and because I insisted on getting stitched up that night, it is still noticeable.

It didn't take me too long to get over it, but I was wondering was this going to be one of those years.

Páirc Uí Chaoimh was opened up that year and we took on Kerry in the first big game to be played at the venue. That Munster final drew a huge crowd and there were some teething problems which resulted in the crowd spilling onto the pitch.

There was no bother from the fans and I wasn't interfered with in any way even though they were right down on top of us and I had to ask the supporters from both counties to step back so I could get my run going for the kick-outs.

The game was one of the best I have played in. The fact the crowd were right around the pitch on the sidelines made it even more exciting. It finished 0-10 apiece and I saved a second-half penalty from Mikey Sheehy in what was a fair result.

The replay was also in Páirc Uí Chaoimh and there was another massive crowd on a very hot and sunny day.

It was a ding-dong battle. Mickey Ned O'Sullivan and Pat Spillane got two goals for Kerry. Seamus Coughlan and Jimmy Barry Murphy scored two for us. JBM intercepted a Kerry clearance for his goal and that put us seven points clear. What's more, we were playing well and I was happy at that stage we would go on to win the game.

John Moloney was the referee and he also did the 1973 All-Ireland final when, of course, we won.

At some stage when the ball was at the other end of the field, one of the umpires said to me: 'Do you remember that goal you said was no goal in '73. You said the ball wasn't behind the line?'

'I do ya,' I said. And we chatted on as the ball was still up near the Kerry goal. I explained to the umpire my reason for making a comment after that '73 final.

'I thought, at the time, the ball hit the post and came back out, but when I saw the picture in the 'Irish Independent' the next day I could see the ball was over the line.'

'Grand,' he said.

The ball was played down the field and Kerry got a free to the left of our goal. Sheehy, clever as ever, took a short one to Seán Walsh who in my opinion was not fully 14 yards from the ball. Seán turned and took a shot.

I was in front of the backs who were on the line, but the ball flew past me. Brian Murphy was standing on the goal-line. I could see his two feet slightly behind the line, but he was crouched over. Brian caught the ball and the umpire put up the green flag for a goal.

I turned to the umpire. 'There's no way the ball is over the line.'

He looked me straight in the eye and said, 'You were wrong in '73 and you're wrong again today.'

That took the wind out of my sails and I didn't say anymore. The goal brought our lead down to a point. To make matters worse, we kicked out the ball and it went all the way down to the other end of the field. Seánie Murphy, who starred on Páidí Ó Sé in both games, floated in a free from 40 yards out and Declan Barron fisted it into the net. I've seen it a thousand times and Declan was not inside the square, but John Moloney disallowed it.

The ref went in to consult with the umpires and I don't know if he changed their minds or if they changed his, but either way the goal was disallowed. It looked to me though as if the referee went in when they were putting up the green flag. Kerry won the kick-out and Pat Spillane scored the equaliser with less than a minute to go.

I kicked out the ball and it finished up with Mikey Sheehy and I groaned 'oh no'. Of all the men to get the ball with time nearly up. Mikey put it straight between the posts, but the point wasn't given by John Moloney who blew for timeup just as the ball was sailing over the bar.

Kerry had won the game and the ref totally chickened out. If right was right, Kerry should have won, but he was trying to balance things out. Whether his conscience was at him over the two terrible decisions or not, it's impossible to tell. We were well beaten in extra-time and it would be an understatement if we said we felt aggrieved.

We were shattered in the dressing room afterwards. I think had we won we might have gone on to win the All-Ireland. Dublin beat Kerry in the final and they were one of the greatest teams of all time, but I felt we could have taken them.

I was 31 and there was a feeling somewhere inside of me that there was still a chance of winning an All-Ireland medal. I had absolutely no notion of retiring.

# CHAPTER 14

## *Earning Our Stripes*

**THERE'S NEVER A DULL MOMENT IN CORK GAA – ESPECIALLY WHEN THE CORK COUNTY BOARD** is involved. Whatever road the Board travels, a good row is almost certain to follow.

In 1977, there was a big split between the players and the Board and it was all for the love of the jersey.

Adidas had given Donie Donovan a set of jerseys for the '76 Munster final. There was no monetary payment and all the players wanted was a jersey; if you got a tracksuit, you'd nearly think you'd won the lottery.

The Adidas jerseys were made in Germany and had the three-stripe Adidas livery, but we gave that get-up absolutely no thought at all in those days before replica kits came in.

The County Board started putting black tape over the Adidas logo in the minutes leading up to the '76 Munster final, but once we started to sweat up a bit, the tape fell off and the Adidas logo was visible. No one took much notice as Adidas hadn't really taken off in Ireland at that stage, except maybe among the younger kids.

At that time, when you played with Cork, you brought down your own boots, socks and knicks. The GAA rule was that all kit had to be Irish-made. There was an investigation, of sorts, by the Board. Adidas were, of course, a German company and we were told 'don't let it happen again', but that was it and it didn't seem like a big deal at the time.

Sometime around the beginning of 1977, Adidas employee Pat Moore, who was the Irish javelin champion, and his MD, Mick O'Connell, made an approach to Dinny Allen in relation to the company providing us with gear. The two lads were Corkmen and Adidas was based in Cork. I was asked to talk to Adidas on behalf of the players.

Adidas offered us jerseys, knicks, boots and tracksuits. All they wanted in return was a photograph of us wearing their gear. The County Board only gave us jerseys. We told Adidas we couldn't wear their jerseys, but that we had no problem with wearing the rest of the kit.

I put it to the selectors and they said they would talk to the County Board. The National League had started up and we were getting no answers. Eventually, we got fed up of waiting. I'm not sure if there was any communication between the County Board and the selectors, but in any case we heard nothing.

It was going on and going on and eventually we went back to Adidas and told them we felt we couldn't wear the jerseys. We made it clear to Adidas that if we got boots, socks, knicks and tracksuits, we would do the team photograph in the gear.

We were kind of waiting then for the championship to see who was on the panel and there was another delay. Cork had a tournament lined up against Mayo in Ruislip in London and before we went Adidas gave us a set of knicks with the three stripes on the side.

I was giving out the togs to fellas in the dressing rooms before the match and Paddy O'Driscoll, who was a selector and a Board man, got very excited. 'Ye can't wear them, ye can't wear them.'

Donie Donovan more or less told him to stop going on about it. I said something like, 'look ye don't give us knicks so we had to get our own. It's none of the Board's business'. JBM was captain. He was only 23 at the time, but he wasn't afraid to speak his mind, though by inclination he was a quiet sort of a fella. JBM backed me up. We wore the knicks in Ruislip.

We were drawn against Clare in the first round of the championship down in Limerick. By now we had new boots and tracksuits – all supplied by Adidas. The full team agreed to a deal whereby we would wear the boots and the top of the tracksuits. In return, we would stand in for a photograph before the game. We weren't wearing the Adidas jerseys at this stage, so we felt we weren't rocking the boat.

I was dealing with Adidas, but we were 100 per cent together and absolutely no pressure was put on any player.

Donie Donovan went to see Big Donal O'Sullivan, the chairman of the County Board, on the day before the match. Donie said he didn't want any trouble over the wearing of the gear. Big Donal said he didn't want any trouble either.

We went on to the pitch wearing Adidas tops and the subs wore both tops and bottoms. The players stood in a straight row for a photograph and the Adidas photographer took a picture of the full squad. We beat Clare handily enough and qualified to meet Kerry in the Munster final.

We started back training the following Tuesday night. The executives of the County Board used to meet in Páirc Uí Chaoimh on a Tuesday night. I was out training and I was asked to go up to the Board meeting in their rooms in the stand.

Dr Con came over and said, 'Billy, whatever you do, hold the head. Don't lose the head.'

I was determined to keep my cool and it was a Board member who lost the head in the end.

He went on the attack. He said, 'Ye footballers are always the same. Ye are always causing trouble, always looking for something'.

I kept cool. 'Most other counties get gear,' I said, 'and we feel left out. We don't want any confrontation with the Board. We only want to train as best we can and do our best to beat Kerry.'

Frank Murphy said, 'Look Billy, we all want to solve this amicably'.

I was happy with that and so were the players.

We didn't hear from the Board so we thought everything was fine, but then after our final training session on the Wednesday night before the Munster final, we had our usual team meeting.

The chairman came into the room at some stage. The five selectors were also present. Unknown to the players, there was a letter on the way threatening us with suspension if we wore the Adidas gear. There wasn't a word said about it at the meeting. I can swear to that.

Donie Donovan was at the meeting too, and he told us afterwards he didn't know about the letter and he didn't. The other four selectors knew the letter was on its way, but not one of them said a word. And of course the chairman knew as well.

We decided on the Wednesday that we would have a kickabout on the Saturday morning before the game. That wasn't our normal procedure. One of the selectors went into a panic and said, 'What's this about training on a Saturday? What's all this for?' He obviously thought we would only come together just before the match when we would be in disarray and would not have had a chance to discuss the letter as a group.

The following day was a Thursday and usually there was a letter from Frank Murphy informing us of the travel arrangements, like as in 'we will meet outside the courthouse at such a time'. That sort of thing.

The letter threatened us with suspension if we wore the Adidas gear. Remember there was no mention of the letter at the final team meeting. And I hadn't heard of any contact from the Board since my meeting with them.

We trained on Saturday as planned and when we finished the session Donie said: 'For what it's worth lads, here's my opinion. I would go along with the Board and wear white knicks and we'll beat Kerry. Then on Tuesday night I'll lead ye into the Board and we'll give them what's what. Now I'm going to leave it up to ye, and if ye decide otherwise, then I'll back ye one hundred per cent.'

Andy Sheehy, who was the chairman of selectors, agreed with what Donie had said even though he didn't say he would lead us into the County Board.

JBM spoke first. 'I agree with Donie,' he said. 'We'll wear the white knicks. We'll beat Kerry and then we will go into see this County Board.' I agreed with JBM.

It was getting a bit cool at this stage and we went into the dressing room to continue the discussion and who should arrive in but one of the selectors.

Not everyone in the room agreed with Donie, JBM and myself. There were dissenting voices among the players.

'Why should we go along with them when they did nothing for us?' And someone else said, 'We have the board over a barrel'. That sort of thing.

The argument was going to and fro, but to be quite honest it looked like the meeting was going to agree with what Donie suggested.

Then, lo and behold, who should open up only the selector.

'As far as I can see,' he said, ' ye are only creepin' and crawlin' trying to get free gear.' I was taking a bandage off my wrist as he was talking, and I threw it at him.

'F\*\*k you,' I said, 'who are you trying to call a creepy-crawly?'

Jimmy Barry Murphy jumped up on a chair and said, 'Tomorrow lads we're wearing the three-stripe togs'. There was no more about it after that and we left the dressing room. I think if the selector hadn't butted in, we wouldn't have worn the three-stripe knicks. Players just want to play and don't need distractions like that so close to big games.

We went to Killarney by train on the Sunday morning of the game. On the way down to Kerry, there were County Board officials with JBM at the end of the carriage trying to persuade him to talk us into wearing the plain white knicks.

From the station we were taken to our hotel and we were asked in the team room if we would wear the white knicks.

JBM spoke first.

'Ye never made it ye're business to look after us. We have done nothing wrong. We are wearing the three-stripe knicks.' The players went with him.

We went out onto the pitch wearing the three-stripe togs and boots, but we wore the plain red jerseys handed to us by the Board.

There was another surprise. Most of the Kerry lads were also wearing the three-stripe gear!

We started well and went six points up, but Kerry wiped us out afterwards. We were all suspended almost immediately. Well, not exactly. JBM and Brian Murphy were also playing with the hurlers and while they were suspended from playing football, they were not banned from playing hurling!

Cork went on to win the All-Ireland hurling title that year.

The strange thing is that the row was never over jerseys. The big battle was over the knicks, but by now there was a feeling the players were very much second-class citizens. There was also the feeling we weren't appreciated. We were all the one and remained very close.

There were more meetings after that and it turned out that even though we were suspended from playing with Cork, we were still playing with our clubs as we were only barred from inter-county football. Cork didn't have any football during the summer and the Board kept the clubs onside by allowing us to play club football and hurling.

There were numerous meetings among the players in a room over Mike Healy's Mall Tavern Bar, but nothing came of it. We met the chairman of the County Board but nothing was resolved. Someone tried to mediate.

It was going nowhere. We were worn down in the end. A couple of weeks before the National League, JBM told me the Board wanted us to sign a letter stating we wouldn't wear the Adidas gear.

We both felt we couldn't win, and we backed down.

I suppose it was in the back of our minds that we had relatively short playing careers. The Board knew this too. Unlike the players, they could carry on in the same jobs for years and years.

If we had a Donal Óg Cusack, we might have kept it going. Maybe if we kept at that battle back in 1977, the troubles of the last few years would have been avoided. We weren't cut out for GAA politics and we probably lacked the confidence of the players of today. There was no union to support us and the players weren't yet properly organised on a national level. And anyway we just wanted to play football.

\* \* \*

Nemo won the county again that year. We beat St Michael's in the final on a dirty, wet day with a big second-half performance against a gale.

We were always a good team against the wind as we worked the ball very well and always kept going right through to the end. There was never any let-up when you wore the Nemo jersey and we were prepared to die out on the pitch for the club. We were always very fit and from an early stage, I realised you couldn't play football if you weren't fit.

That was our fourth county since 1972 and I trained all four teams.

And Munster won the Railway Cup again.

Mick O'Dwyer was manager in two of the years when I played with Munster. Micko wasn't going to give away any management tips and he said the same thing to us both years – 'Lads, ye are the best team around. Go out and prove that' – but he did command great respect, even if he did keep the secrets of Kerry football to himself!

# CHAPTER 15

# *One In, All In*

THE GAA COMMUNITY IS A VERY SMALL PLACE. YOU TOG OUT WITH YOUR CLOSE FRIENDS AND neighbours and there are often huge overlaps between fellas you played with and against in the club, the school or the county.

In my own case, we often kept it all in the family.

In 1978, for example, Frank Cogan was appointed as Cork manager/coach by the Cork selectors. Ray Cummins, who was married to Mary's sister Bernadette, hadn't played with us for a couple of years, but he came back out of retirement. Frank was married to Mary's twin sister Anne! We all got on very well together and still do. We were friends even before we became in-laws.

However, it didn't do us any good in the Munster final against Kerry. We went into that match reasonably confident, as we did every year against Kerry, but we were beaten by 3-14 to 3-7. It was the usual story and we missed a few easy scores.

Eugene Desmond, whom I taught and trained in Sully's Quay, came in at full-back. Kerry played another young lad at full-forward – the Bomber Liston.

I knew the Bomber as a kid from the times when a gang from Nemo used to go Ballybunion on holidays. We used to drink in his parents' pub and I remember this small boy running up and down the stairs: The Bomber. In the years that followed we got to know each other very well indeed!

He was the final piece in the jigsaw for that great Kerry team and he was lethal that day in his first Munster final.

Mick O'Dwyer was under pressure that year. There was speculation he was on his last chance. Kerry had just lost twice in a row to Dublin and in Kerry there's no mercy for beaten managers. If we had taken our scores in that first quarter, you'd never know what might have happened. The course of football history might have been very different.

I won my fourth Railway Cup with most of that Kerry team and we won our fifth county final, once again against St Michael's.

Frank played corner-back and he was outstanding. Even though he was getting on a bit, he still had a serious burst of pace. The young players were coming through. Jimmy Kerrigan played that year with us as did Timmy Dalton, who was probably the best club player in Cork. Jimmy got his place on the Cork team and did well on Pat Spillane in the Munster final.

I wouldn't be too sure when it started to change for Nemo, but it was probably around then. The county was hoping for another team to win and we were no longer the underdogs. Nemo had become the team to beat. And of course the Cork County Board hadn't gone away either.

Kerry went on to win the All-Ireland in '78, scoring five goals in the final and Charlie Nelligan, the Kerry goalie was sent off. The All-Star rules stated that if you were sent off you were not eligible for selection and so Charlie was unlucky. I was told on good authority I was to be the All-Star goalkeeper.

Someone tipped me off that Con Murphy, who was a former secretary of the Cork County Board, and then president of the GAA, stopped my selection. This was no doubt payback for my role in the three-stripe controversy.

There was more chastisement on the way.

In late 1978, at the start of the National League, Frank Cogan asked me if I would coach and train the team. The other selectors were for it and the proposal went before the County Board. The Board knocked it.

The then-chairman Paddy O'Driscoll, who was of course a central figure in the three-stripe affair, stated at the meeting that he didn't like my methods of training. How would he know? Paddy never saw me train Nemo. He wasn't at a single training session, nor did he ever ask me about my training methods. More payback.

Some of the selectors, including Frank, said they would have no option but to resign if I wasn't appointed. They saw the move as a vote of no confidence in me.

The papers picked up on it and an internal dispute in Cork was out in the open.

The last thing I wanted was trouble with the Board. All I wanted to do was train the team for the good of Cork football. They had no football reason to veto my selection. My record with Nemo and Sully's Quay spoke for itself.

There was a proposal that Frank would continue to coach the team and I would become trainer. Presumably, this meant I would do physical training with the squad and Frank would be in charge of tactics.

I agreed and the Board accepted the compromise.

The so-called solution was only a joke anyway, as Frank Cogan and myself were like brothers. The reality was that I took over the coaching as well as the training, but with a major input from Frank. We shared the same views on the game and, of course, the bond between us was forged in primary school. I had absolutely no say in selection which is the way I wanted it, as I was still a player.

We got off to a good start that autumn and beat Kerry in our first match of the 1978-79 National League. We played really well. Kevin Kehilly did a good job on 'The Bomber' and Dinny Allen was outstanding. The score was 2-10 to 2-5.

Now that game obviously meant more to us than Kerry, but I knew from the way we played and I knew from our attitude that we were a good team. You have to have faith and I had plenty.

Cork had a very good run to the league final through 1978 and into 1979. We came up against Roscommon in my first national final as trainer. That was a very, very good Roscommon team and they beat us well in what was probably their best ever display. That same Roscommon team should probably have beaten Kerry in the following year's All-Ireland final if they had concentrated on playing football.

It was a setback for us, but we gained valuable experience. We played in a national final in Croke Park. Roscommon had one of those days when everything goes just right. We didn't expect to lose that one. Confidence was high going in and possibly we might have been a bit over-confident, but Roscommon would have beaten anyone on the day.

We were reasonably confident going into the Munster final against Kerry, but we missed two penalties in Killarney – one in each half. Everything has to be 100 per cent right on the day if you want to beat Kerry. You just cannot afford to miss chances.

We weren't that far away in the finish. Mick O'Dwyer came into our dressing room after the game as he did every year and said the very same thing. 'Lads, don't be too downhearted. Ye are the second best team in the country.'

It was torture having to listen to him.

I was just sitting down in the dressing room with my head down muttering profanities to myself and I felt like throwing a boot at him. I couldn't even look at him.

We used to train like dogs for the Munster final and we always thought some day we could catch Kerry off guard. Years later, Mikey Sheehy, who by then had become a close friend, told me they trained as hard for the Munster final as if it was their first All-Ireland.

It always annoys me when I hear people who had no clue as to just how much we put into trying to beat Kerry say that Kerry had it soft against us. This was a terrible insult to Cork. I can tell you this. I never played on a Cork team that ever gave anything soft to anyone. We always had great pride in the Cork jersey, and wouldn't let the jersey down no matter what. Kerry would never have been as good if we hadn't pushed them so hard early on in the year. We exposed any deficiencies they might have had and they got nothing easy from us. It was dog-eat-dog in those Cork-Kerry clashes and if there was any weakness in you, it would be exposed in front of forty or fifty thousand people.

The Cork footballers of that era never gave up and there's credit due to them for that. It's easy to keep on going when you're winning. There was no back door back then and we trained for months for just two games.

* * *

I was still coaching Nemo and we won the county and Munster club championships. We were up against Killererin of Galway on their home pitch for the All-Ireland club semi.

There was a patch of waste ground of about 40 or 50 yards in front of the old Nemo clubhouse. We used to train there in the bad weather. We had no floodlights but we took advantage of the spillover from the lights in the clubhouse.

There was a big article about Killererin in one of the papers, and it was all about the small country club against the big city club. There was a photograph accompanying the piece and it showed Killererin training under full floodlights. Nemo were still trying to improve their facilities. We had come from playing on Corporation pitches to owning our own field, but we knew we had to keep on improving our grounds. There were two sides to the club. Playing obviously was one side, but the men and women who managed the running of the club were as much a part of our success as the players.

Again we used 'what it says in the papers' to motivate the players. We were the underdogs as far as we were concerned and we travelled to Galway with that in mind.

Killererin couldn't have been more hospitable. They didn't know what to do for us and our supporters. We were clapped onto the pitch – and belted off it. It was a savage battle, although I must say I enjoyed every minute of it. We escaped with a win and once the match was over Killererin resumed the hospitality.

Nemo always stood up for themselves. We never tried to carry a player who wouldn't give one hundred per cent. It was one in, all in. And Frank Cogan's statement 'you'd never see a Nemo man on his own' was always in the back of our minds. That carried on to the field of play. You never had to watch your back playing for Nemo.

We went on to play Scotstown of Monaghan in the All-Ireland Club final. We went up to Dublin the night before the match and the heating system in the hotel broke down. I will never forget the cold. It was colder in Dublin that night than it was in Moscow.

I was rooming with our masseur, the legendary Kid Cronin and Cork dual star Brian Murphy. We had coats and jumpers on, but we were still frozen. It was so bad we couldn't get to sleep. The three of us hopped into the one bed for the heat and I wonder what story would have gone out if anyone walked in. There was ferocious slagging from the Nemo gang the next day, and for a long time after that, but at least we were warm. What was that I said again about Nemo and one in, all in?

The cold spell continued into the next day. It was snowing before the match, and it got much worse as the game went on. At one stage I couldn't see the Canal End from my goal on the Hill 16 end. Frank and myself, the old pros on the team, prepared a bottle of brandy and port and we took a good swig before we went out. We took another drop at half-time. Dinny Allen was so cold he took a big drink out of it as well.

We scored a crucial goal and Jimmy Barrett took the credit for it. There was the usual team meeting on the Thursday night before the match. I had the stats on the Monaghan boys, and we went through their team. We even had a Monaghan newspaper with a big write-up on Scotstown. The local reporters would always praise their own team and it was a great way of getting your team going. Jimmy Barrett always had a very singular view on tactics.

'I might just make a point,' he said at the team meeting. Jimmy stood up as if to emphasise the importance of what he was going to say. 'The photograph of Scotstown in the semi-final shows their goalie wearing a woollen hat with a tassle on it.'

I asked Jimmy to explain what he meant.

'He doesn't look too hot, does he with that hat?'

'And so?' I asked, none the wiser.

'The hat isn't quite the right article of clothing for a 'keeper. It's unprofessional and, in my opinion, it's possible we might catch him out with a random shot.'

The lads laid into him and the slagging was ferocious, but Jimmy stuck to his guns.

We had the wind and won a ball out towards the left half-forward position and Timmy Dalton just hit a speculative kick towards goals.

The Scotstown 'keeper came out from his goal, the ball bounced over his head and into the net. Now as it happened he was a very good 'keeper and was probably caught out by the cold as the ball hadn't been up that end for a few minutes. Obviously no one had given him the medicinal drop of brandy and port. We went on to win the All-Ireland for the second time.

And the slagging went on.

Dinny Allen said, 'Hey Billy, you're not coaching us anymore, just show Jimmy a photograph of the opposition.'

Castlehaven beat us in the Cork county championship.

It was nearly as difficult to get out of Cork as it was to win the All-Ireland. The downside of winning the All-Ireland club is that it's very hard to keep up the fitness levels.

And the three-in-a-bed slagging went on all year long.

# CHAPTER 16

# *The Worst Days Of My Life*

I WAS VERY HAPPY IN SULLY'S QUAY. IT WAS A GREAT SCHOOL. DISCIPLINE WAS GOOD. I HAD my dream job. There was the physical education side of it and then there was the teaching aspect. It was a perfect mix.

I knew from back to the time of my mother's death that life can change in an instant. There was a disciplinary issue with one of my pupils. I lost my temper with the young lad and roughed him up.

A complaint was made to the Gardaí and the case came to court in 1980. I was convicted. The judge fined me £40.

In a way it was relief just to get it over with but the weeks and months that followed were a nightmare. It was a very stressful time. I was waiting around for a year for the case to come up. My career was on the line and all over a flash of temper.

And I knew it would make the 'papers because of who I was.

Naturally enough, the 'papers did pick up on it when the case did come to court. I was dying with embarrassment. I was devastated.

We had a game against the Nick's on the evening after the court case out in Ballinlough. I was in two minds whether to play or not. I didn't feel like stirring outside the door, never mind playing a match. It was a county championship game and I didn't want to let the club down. So I said, 'Right, I'll face this now'.

I played and none of the Nick's said a word to me. Fair play to them for that. It was the hardest thing I ever had to do. We won the match and I didn't let in any goal.

My colleagues in Sully's Quay couldn't have been more supportive. I will never forget the back-up they gave me and that was a great help in what were the worst days of my life. I didn't lose my job, but from then on my attitude to teaching changed completely. I decided it wasn't for me but I stayed on in Sully's Quay.

We won the Frewen Cup with the school that year. I think the young lads did it to give me a boost. I remember coming on to the bus after the game and the team clapped me. I nearly broke down. I spoke to them. 'It's been a very difficult year in school for me. Thanks for winning the Frewen. This is a huge boost for me. Thank you for today and for your efforts all year.'

Their support kept me going. I didn't have any real problems with discipline in the school after that incident. Certainly none of the kids ever mentioned it and I had a good relationship with my pupils.

Looking back on it, I was stupid to do what I did. I liked teaching, but my temper let me down at times. Nothing anyone said or did could turn back the clock.

* * *

Cork had a reasonably good year in 1979. We reached the national league final and we were the only team to give Kerry a game of it for over two years.

There was no objection this time to my being appointed coach as well as trainer. The 'Barrs were county champions so Frank Cogan had to step down as a selector as the 'Barrs controlled the selection committee, as was the way back then.

Andy Sheehy from the 'Barrs came in as chairman of selectors. He wanted me as coach and we got on very well. Andy was a gentleman and he always put Cork before club in his year as chairman.

By now, I was getting the players to play my way. I planned carefully and made detailed notes after every game. I made sure each and every player knew what was expected of him. My way was to keep it simple and I didn't overdo the coaching.

I wasn't a selector, but Andy ensured my views were known and for the most part they were taken on board by the selectors with whom I had a good working relationship. Andy made my job very easy.

There wasn't much I didn't know about our opponents in the League final of 1980. We were up against Kerry and of course no one gave us a chance against the Golden Years team.

'Thank God, Mikey Sheehy wasn't fit for selection,' I thought to myself when I heard the Kerry team.

I was always a little bit superstitious. In my speech before the game, I told the lads I felt the omens were all in our favour. 'I won everything at the second attempt. My All-Ireland medal, my Sigerson medal, my county medal, my Railway Cup medal and now I've been beaten in a league final, and what's this, it's the second league final.' There was no shouting, or roaring. I said it nice and calmly and I think what I said definitely got through to the players. Donie Donovan's methods were my guide.

We did win it, by a single point, in what was a great game of football before a full house in Killarney.

We played above ourselves and what made it even sweeter was that Kerry were good on the day. We just played that little bit better.

It was my first national title as coach. And of course I now had the full set of two national titles as a player. I was 35 years of age and I was beginning to wonder if I would ever win the league. I was picked as GAA personality of the month and that gave me great personal satisfaction despite the opposition to me from within my own County Board.

The league win was sweet but we still had to get the better of Kerry in the Munster final. There was a ten-week break between the league final and the Munster final and the gap was probably too long. We started well enough, but it was the same old story. We were beaten by Kerry. Beaten? They hockeyed us.

We had now lost six Munsters in a row against our old enemy.

The Cork players were a great bunch. They did everything I asked of them. There was plenty of spirit around and plenty of talent, but nothing ever really went our way. We never had that little bit of luck you need to beat a really good team.

Once again the 'Barrs beat us in the county. God only knows how many we would have won but for the 'Barrs. They were the makings of us though.

\* \* \*

I had enough of teaching by now . I planned ahead and there was an exit strategy. It was always in my mind to go the States. I wanted to continue my education and I got in touch with Brian Mullins and Fran Ryder, Dubs and footballers who were good friends. The boys were doing their Masters in Physical Education in New York.

I discussed it with Mary and we put plans in place to emigrate. Mary was brilliant throughout and anyway she was every bit as adventurous as I was. My burning interest was in training and coaching teams. I wanted to learn as much as I could. The Masters had nothing to do with career or more money; for me it was all about becoming a better trainer and coach.

\* \* \*

Kerry were going for four All-Irelands in a row in 1981 and we came up against them in the Munster final.

I have very little memory of the game – for a very good reason – but I'm told it was a tough one.

Just after half-time, a high ball came in over our full-back, Kevin Kehilly. I ran out about ten yards for the ball.

The Bomber Liston came running in at top speed. By now he had filled out, and was all muscle. The Bomber was six foot three and he was surely fifteen stone. My eyes were totally on the ball. There was a collision and the next thing I remember is waking up in hospital. I had received 11 stitches, had concussion and a broken collarbone. The Bomber hadn't a mark on him. I was taken by ambulance to Cork and I was in hospital by six o'clock that evening. I spent three days there recovering.

That was my seventeenth Munster final and it was a record. Frank Cogan called in to see me and told me there was another record as well.

'What was that Frank?' I asked weakly.

'It was the earliest you were ever home from Killarney.'

I spent the summer strapped up and there was no football for Nemo until the county final.

I have often been asked if I blamed The Bomber for my injuries. In other words, did he go for me?

The clash was completely accidental. The Bomber went for the ball. I went for the ball. I got there just a fraction before him. He couldn't stop in time. He was bigger than me. I came off worse. It's as simple as that.

Injured or not, I still managed to do a bit of work that summer. My right-hand man in Nemo Jim Cremin and myself were employed by another Nemo stalwart Dommy Daly to sell hams, sausages and rashers around West Cork. We were supplied with a van. There was very little by way of sales and we returned the van in much the same way as it was given to us.

Dommy looked into the van and asked us, 'Is it how ye thought ye were two tourists doing a bit of sightseeing.'

On another occasion, Dommy was asked if we were still working for him.

'Oh yeah. They are alright. They're just taking the hams for a spin.'

I gave up the job of player-coach with Cork in September of 1981. I found the whole thing just a bit too much to handle. I had my mind made up to go to the States to do the Masters.I suppose I didn't take college that seriously but the science and preparation of teams had always been my passion. I couldn't wait to get to New York and the masters.

It wouldn't have been fair to Cork to hang on and at least the new coach would have plenty of time to plan ahead. I was 36 and I wanted to concentrate on playing for the few years I had left with Cork.

Back as far as 1977, I planned to go to Berkeley in California. It was always my dream. Mullins and Ryder came good. I was accepted in NYU for a Masters in Physical Education. I took a career break from teaching. There was no turning back.

The clash with The Bomber didn't affect my confidence. It was part of the game. I was captain of Nemo that year. I missed the county semi-final against the 'Barrs, but I was back for the final against Bantry Blues.

By now, Mickey Niblock from Derry had joined us. He was a top-class player and a really nice man. His son David plays with us now. David, of course, also played with distinction for Cork. We won the county final and it was a sweet one for me as I was captain as well as coach and trainer.

I played my last competitive match for Cork in Páirc Uí Chaoimh against Dublin in November of 1981 and we lost. I was nearly 37 and after 17 years playing for Cork, it was time to go. I made no fuss over the retirement and didn't tell anyone it was my last game. I was somewhat emotional inside as I walked off the pitch, but I kept myself to myself.

That was the way I wanted it.

I then played what I thought was my last game for Nemo in the first round of the Munster club championship. That was that as far as I was concerned. I was retired from Cork and Nemo.

There was a rumour doing the rounds that I was fired because of the incident with the young lad. That wasn't true. I took leave of absence. I had my fill of teaching, but at the same time it was always on my mind that some day I would like to go to the States. The incident with the young fella just accelerated it.

# CHAPTER 17

# A Brand New Start Of It

**WE LEFT FOR AMERICA FROM SHANNON ON THE 16TH OF JANUARY, 1982. BRIAN WAS SEVEN,** Alan was only two and here we were heading off for New York. Mary was all for it. She always supported me in everything I did.

My passion was training teams and I wanted to learn as much as I could about physical preparation. The course I finally decided on was a Masters in Fitness Management.

Colm Drumgoole picked me up at the airport. He was a Vincent's man and as I have said we had a very good relationship with them. We had some great nights with the Drumgooles in Dublin and Colm's mother Péig hosted the best of parties back in her house.

Now before coming over, Jimmy Sweeney from Kilnamartyra asked me if I would play for the Carlow Club in New York which he was involved with. Jimmy Kerrigan and Timmy Dalton had been over to play with them and had given me good reports. It was normal to play with clubs that had a different title to your own county. There was quite a few Kerry lads playing for Carlow and they made me very welcome.

Carlow promised to get me a job and an apartment. The apartment wasn't ready when we arrived, but Colm took me up to Brian Mullins' apartment in The Bronx. Mullins, of course, was another Vincent's man and one of the greatest Gaelic footballers of all time. Again the GAA network came good. Brian's wife Helen welcomed us and marked our card.

We spent our first week in New York with the Dubs.

Carlow still hadn't managed to find an apartment, but they put us up with Tilly and Noel McPartland who couldn't have been nicer to us. I stayed with Tilly and Noel until such time as we got fixed up a few weeks later. Our apartment was in Woodside in Queens, a predominantly Irish neighbourhood. The economy in Ireland was in bad shape at the time and thousands of Irish emigrated to the

States in the seventies and early eighties. There were parts of New York that were every bit as Irish as Ireland. Woodside was one of those areas.

Carlow fixed me up with temporary jobs – mostly bartending – until finally I got sorted with a position in a bar called Goodfellas on Second Avenue. I started to play out the field with Carlow at training and I was delighted with the change. Unfortunately, I only played one match with the club. There was some dispute, which had nothing to do with me, and we were thrown out of the championship.

* * *

My new vocation as a barman took a bit of getting used to.

The way out there was for the barmen to be chatty, but I just served up the drink and said nothing. I suppose I was a bit shy and being new to the city, I wasn't sure what to say or do.

I got the bullet from Goodfellas – not as bad as it sounds! – after about six weeks. And the reason I was given was that I was too quiet.

Fran and Brian were working in a bar called Rosie O'Grady's. I used to spend a lot of time up there with the two boys and I got to know the owners, Austin Delaney and Mike Carthy. Brian was going home and I was given his job in Rosie O'Grady's.

Brian wasn't playing at the time as he had a bad car accident in Ireland before he came out to the States but Fran was playing for Leitrim. Mike Carthy was heavily involved with them. Three or four of the bartenders were playing with the club and they were a very good team.

I decided to join up with Leitrim as well. I played senior hurling with Clare as well as junior hurling with Cork and they had chipped in with Carlow to pay my fare out. There were times when the hurling in New York could be tough enough, but I enjoyed every minute of it. Clare were very good to me. The Clare team talks were hilarious.

'Go out there and give them plenty of timber. Drive 'em into the ground. Cut the heads off 'em. I want to see blood spilt.' Then just before we went out on the pitch, the trainer blessed himself. 'Now lads, we'll all say a prayer that no one will be hurt.'

Martin O'Doherty, who had played senior hurling and football with Cork, had been out in Los Angeles and he called to see me in New York. Martin was to stay with me for a night, but there was a blizzard and he ended up staying three nights. Martin asked me if we would go back home if Cork came calling for us to play in the All-Ireland championship. I think the two of us felt there wasn't a hope in hell of that happening.

Martin was asked to return and he did, but I wasn't asked to go back.

By now, I was settled in New York. Rosie's was a good place to work. Mary was very happy. The kids had settled in well and there was no shortage of Irish in our neighbourhood. The apartment was what was known as a 'railway apartment'. The reason it was called a railway apartment was that you had to go through one bedroom to get into another, just like railway carriages.

We had our share of callers and lodgers. I put up a good few past pupils and Nemo boys. That was the way with the Irish in New York. You'd never see anyone stuck. Some of the lads ended up staying a couple of months until they got fixed up with their own places.

Leitrim were looking for players. I got in touch with the McCarthy brothers, Vincie and Pat, and they joined the club. Anthony Delaney, who was also from Bantry, joined up as well. The three boys were living in Boston and Leitrim brought them down to New York for the matches. We had some great laughs with those three lads who always stayed with us when they were in the city.

Mary was well able to cope with all this. She loved the company. I suppose the fact she was reared in a hotel was a big help. Mary never complained and always made the lads welcome. By now Brian started at school and he settled in well.

I was earning good money in Rosie's. Mary was working as a waitress in a diner and she liked her job. The kids were happy and we had a good life of it. There were holidays to Florida and weekends in the Catskills. We were part of the Irish community in New York.

We didn't mix much outside of the Irish community and didn't make that many new American friends. The Irish in New York had built up a support network and a way of life that made the city as Irish as they could possibly manage.

There were pitfalls too and many fell by the wayside. I was working in Goodfellas one day when one of the barmen asked this down and out to leave. I couldn't help but notice that the barman gave the drunk five dollars as he put him out.

'What's the story with your man?' I asked.

'You mean you don't know him, Billy? That guy won an All-Ireland senior medal.' And he told me the misfortune's name. I knew him well, but didn't recognise him in his dishevelled state. The down and out came out on a GAA trip and told his friends he was staying on for a while. I think it might have been a spur-of-the-moment thing. He became hooked on the drink and finished up on Skid Row.

There were three good GAA lads who came into Rosie's and they looked after him as best they could.

Every now and then they would get him off the sauce. The lads cleaned him up and sorted him out with a job, but then a few weeks later he would break out and would be as bad as ever. It was a very sad situation and while most of the Irish prospered, many fell through the cracks.

I mixed study with family life and work. The masters entailed a fair bit of effort but I loved what I was doing. NYU was a great place to study. The course was at the cutting edge. It wasn't as if I was forcing myself to study and I duly passed my Masters.

* * *

There was bad news from home in the summer of 1983. Tom Creedon died from injuries he suffered in an accident. It was a terrible shock. I was very friendly with Tom. I do know he respected me greatly as a coach. He would give you everything he had on the pitch.

Tom was very loyal and a great team player.

He died the night Cork were beaten by Dublin in the All-Ireland semi-final. Tom was a very upstanding kind of a fella. You could trust him with your life.

\* \* \*

I had a lot more time on my hands now that I was finished studying and going to lectures. In a way, I missed the course and NYU. It was all that I hoped it would be. The plan was that I might go back to Ireland and use the Masters to get a job at a higher level, such as in one of the universities or in one of the new Regional Colleges. I learned so much about every aspect of training teams from physiology to psychology and I was already applying what I had learned to Gaelic football and soccer.

That was the real reason we had come to New York.

I won a World Cup medal in 1984. Well, sort of. There was a Welcome Home festival in Ballina and New York entered a team. There were teams from Australia, North America and London for what was an extremely enjoyable few days. I was back in goal by now and we won what was titled 'the World Cup' when New York beat London in the final.

Shamrocks, my soccer team, were on tour at the same time and I travelled down to Cork to play with them. It was my second trip home since I left. I went back a year previously to see Nemo play in the county final. Luckily, I was on a student visa and I could come and go as I pleased. Victor Bennett was manager of that Shamrocks team. He was on the Scoil Chríost Rí team with me when we won the Under-13 city schools title. He was very good to me in the States.

In fact, I ended up as player-manager of Shamrocks.

I managed to fit in the 1984 All-Ireland hurling final in Thurles between Cork and Offaly after the 'World Cup' win. It was the centenary year of the GAA and the All-Ireland hurling captains were introduced to the crowd. I got to thinking they would do the same for the footballers and hoped it might mean another trip home.

I went back to New York, but I heard nothing from the County Board. That surprised me as I was the only surviving Cork All-Ireland winning football captain.

John O'Driscoll, the secretary of Nemo, got in touch and told me he would contact the County Board. The Board decided they would not pay my fare back home. Nemo continued to press the Board. The club really wanted to see their man in Croke Park. John called me a few days later. The County Board had agreed to pay a third of the fare, Nemo would come up with a third and, he wondered, would I pay the rest? I was delighted and agreed to the compromise. Nemo were playing in the All-Ireland seven-a side championship that weekend and I met up with the boys in Thurles.

John handed me over their third of the fare which I had already paid myself. To this day, I have never been paid the County Board's share. I couldn't be bothered my arse begging them for it.

\* \* \*

Another year passed by in New York, and in 1985 I wrote to Sully's Quay for an extension to my leave of absence. The Department of Education refused my application. I was told if I wanted to keep my job, I would have to start teaching again in September of 1985.

We gave serious thought to remaining on in New York. I think if we didn't have kids at the time, we might have stayed a while longer, or maybe even for good. Brian was 11 and Alan was six. The post at home was permanent, but we had good jobs in New York. It was a tough decision.

I missed Nemo and my family back home, but since the incident with the young lad and the subsequent court case, teaching never meant the same to me.

In the end, we decided to come home. And back to teaching.

Many Irish people living at home seem to think New York is like some sort of a jail sentence. You're an emigrant and therefore you must be unhappy. You miss home for sure and many who went had no choice but to leave as there was no work at home. But we loved our time in New York and we go back whenever we can to meet our friends. The people over there would do anything for you. In many ways, they are more aware of their Irish heritage than we are here at home. I suppose we take it for granted, whereas the Irish communities in the States see the GAA as a way of keeping up their identity in the melting pot that is New York.

We went back to our old house and the boys went to school in Douglas, near where we lived.

It was also back to school for me in September. I was given what I thought was a perfect timetable. It was all Physical Education. Great, I thought, no exam classes, no corrections and no research.

That worked out fine for a while, but then I began to envy the other teachers who were correcting copies in the staff room. I had nothing to work towards. The greatest thing about teaching is when you put in a big effort and you see the kids improve as the year goes on.

I was still running. Mick O'Connell, my old pal from the three-stripe affair, had asked me if I would run for charity in the Cork City Marathon which was on the following Sunday. Another friend Frank Brady had got me into running in New York. We used to run around the lakes near Flushing Meadows, or up in Van Courtland Park . I took it up again when I came home. I always kept fit. I was 41 now, but I was training as hard as ever. Keeping in shape had become a way of life. I was still fit enough to play football. I hadn't done any marathon training but I did manage to complete the race in three hours and 51 minutes.

I trained with Nemo the day after the marathon even though I was absolutely wrecked.

Dinny Allen was captain of the Nemo intermediate hurling team at the time and he signed me up. We had a league game on the Sunday before the first round of the intermediate county championship.

I went up for the ball and the player marking me struck me straight down on the top of the head with the hurley. I was carted off and had to get five stitches.

'That's it,' said Mary when she saw the state of me, 'you're not playing any more hurling.'

I agreed with her.

We were due to play Midleton the following Sunday in the first round of the intermediate championship. Mary went to Mass on her own and she ran into Dinna Driscoll and his wife Pat, who unfortunately passed away a few years later. Dinna is a great Nemo man and played in the '76 Munster Senior final. Dinna and Pat gave Mary a lift home.

Pat remarked to Mary, 'What do you think of my fella going off playing a hurling match today?'

'Thanks be to God,' said Mary, 'my fella is retired.'

Later that day, I smuggled out my gear, unknown to Mary, and I went down to Midleton for the match. Nemo brought me on as a sub just before half-time. Now I was never one for hurling helmets. I didn't like wearing them. Maybe I should have!

At the start of the second half, a Midleton player struck me with his hurley and caught me in the forehead. The strike was completely accidental, but within a few seconds I was covered in blood.

Brian was on the sideline with the Nemo lads. 'Brian,' I said, 'whatever you do, don't tell your mother about this.'

I was taken to the hospital and had ten stitches inserted in my forehead.

We went back to Nemo for a few pints. Mary came to collect me. Young Brian kept quiet about the blow, but there was a big plaster over my eye and across my forehead. There was no hiding it. I was caught. That was definitely the end of my hurling career.

Nemo were out of the football championship and I headed back to New York and Rosie's for the rest of the summer. It was as if I had never left. The kids were still in school in Ireland and I stayed with Colm Drumgoole until Mary and the two boys came over.

We rented an apartment in Woodside and we had a lovely summer in New York. The highlight was when I went to see the Steve Cruz-Barry McGuigan world title fight in Las Vegas. The heat at ringside was unbearable, even for the spectators. McGuigan did his best, but he never had a chance in that heat.

# CHAPTER 18

# *Walking The Line*

**MY DAYS IN THE CORK JERSEY WERE OVER BUT THE LURE OF INTER-COUNTY FOOTBALL WAS** impossible to resist.

The Cork selectors contacted me in the autumn of 1986 and asked me if I would coach the Cork senior team. I accepted their offer. It had always been my ambition to train my county and I felt I could do a good job. I wasn't appointed a selector, but we agreed that I could suggest players to the selectors. There were two players at the top of my list.

Dinny Allen hadn't played with Cork for over two years. He was playing great football with Nemo and I felt he was easily good enough.

Dave Barry was another man I wanted in the panel. His story was complicated by the fact that he was playing soccer for Cork City. Now Cork had a code of conduct at the time which stated that players should not play any other sports while they were involved with Cork.

Davy was out of work, he was engaged and building a new house. Cork City were paying Davy, but he agreed to give his first commitment to GAA, if there was a clash of fixtures.

'If I'm off,' he said, 'I want to play with Cork City.'

I could see nothing wrong with that in the circumstances. The Cork County Board saw it differently and my request to put Davy on the panel was turned down.

I tried to get Davy into the panel again in the spring of 1987. I arranged a meeting between Davy and the Cork selectors. It was coming up to the start of the championship and the meeting took place in the stands in Páirc Uí Chaoimh after a Cork practice match.

We had a meeting before the meeting, as often happens in the GAA.

'Davy,' I said, 'if they don't mention the soccer, don't bring it up.'

I made sure I sat opposite Davy in the stand. He would be able to see my facial expressions and nods during the meeting with the selectors.

Frank Murphy was on the selection committee. Davy was asked if he would give a full commitment to Cork, and he said he would. The meeting was going very well and was just about to wind up when Davy said, 'I just want to bring something up.'

'Go on,' said Frank.

'Ye brought in a rule that I can't play soccer on my Sundays off. Now I want to play with City when there's no football on.'

I cringed. Davy wasn't included in the panel.

Dinny Allen was always very witty and he christened Dave with a new name. 'From now on Davy, we're going to call you George Washington -'I cannot tell a lie'.'

The selectors wouldn't wear Dinny either. I was very disappointed, but I just got on with it and we started training.

I had my first training session with the Cork panel on a Saturday afternoon in October, just after the start of the National League. The players lacked confidence.

Frank Murphy could be very critical of players whom he felt were not performing. That was just his approach and while it works for some coaches, it was not my way.

I took the lads away over to the far side of the pitch – away from the selectors. I told them not to worry about the sideline. That was my job and I would look after that side of things.

'All ye have to do,' I told them, 'is to look after what happens on the pitch.'

I think that gave the players confidence straight away. Frank was a very strong voice in the selection committee and I knew I had to find a way of dealing with him. You needed him on your side as he wielded huge influence in the day-to-day running of the County Board. His title was nominally County Secretary, but he was really Chief Executive, and he was in everything except the crib at Christmas. Frank was in a very strong position as he was a permanent fixture on the board, whereas the chairmen and the other County Board officers had to be changed every few years.

He liked to get his own way and he usually did. The big thing was that I would be training my native county and I would have to find some way of dealing with Frank. Dinny McDonnell gave me very good advice on how to handle Frank.

'I never had any problem with Frank,' Dinny told me. 'You have to be strong with him. Just tell him what you're doing and don't ask his permission, just do it.'

Frank was very efficient and did whatever I asked, but I was always firm with him. Instead of saying something like, 'Frank, could you please organise a bus for Dublin?', I would just tell Frank I wanted a bus. You had to be strong and I think he respected that.

UCC also approached me to train their Sigerson Cup team. It suited me fine. The Sigerson would be held during the winter break in the National League. We trained at lunchtime or in the afternoons and it didn't interfere with Cork, or Nemo.

Mick O'Dwyer's son John was captain of UCC and we hit it off almost immediately. He was a good lad with a lovely attitude towards the game. We shocked Queen's in the first round. Trinity were next up in the semi-final and we won that handy enough. Jordanstown had a star-studded team and we were big outsiders in the final. They were managed by the late Eamonn Coleman who went on to manage Derry to win the All-Ireland.

We went to Mass on the morning of the match. The sermon had something to do with the Kingdom and I said to the lads, 'That's it now, God is with us. The sermon was all about the Kingdom and we have a Kerry captain.'

We went down by a point. The lads gave it everything. It was just that we were beaten by a better team, barely. It was a huge disappointment, but the Sigerson hadn't changed that much from my time and we stopped in several pubs on the way home in the bus. I have to say I enjoyed myself very much.

There was one thing that stuck in my head. During the course of that long journey home from the Sigerson, my new friend, young John O'Dwyer said to me, 'Bill, I can see yourself and the father having some right battles in the summer.' How right he was.

\* \* \*

**BOY ZONE:** *Lining out with my mates on The Pitch in Tonyville Terrace, Cork. Back row, left to right: Corny Sheehan, Pat O'Connor, Dave Osborne, Donal Scully, John Rafferty and Martin Scully. Front row: Ger Thornhill, Eddie Brophy, myself, Donie O'Brien and Tony O'Callaghan*

**GENERATION GAME:** *My dad Tom and my son Brian*

**BUTTER WOULDN'T MELT...** *My brothers Noel and Tony and sister Mary*

**RUFF JUSTICE:** *Mary, Tony, Noel and myself in the arms of my mother Sheila, with our dog Rory*

**TASTE FOR SUCCESS:** *With the Scoil Chríost Rí Under-13s in 1956. Frank Cogan has ball in hand*

**SOLID GROUNDING:** *Captaining the Coláiste Chríost Rí Frewen Cup team. Back row, left to right: John Canniffe, John Cawley, John Cogan, Mick Healy, Donal Lyne, Tom Martin, Tadgh Cotter and Liam Connolly. Front row: Liam Brady, Ray Twomey, Brendan Tynan, myself, John O'Leary, Pat O'Brien and John O'Boyle*

**TAKING THE MICKO:** *Making a save in the 1968 Munster final in Killarney as Mick O'Dwyer, who came out of retirement to score points from all angles in Kerry's 1-21 to 3-8 victory, looks on*

**OH CAPTAIN, MY CAPTAIN:** *The 1973 All-Ireland club final presentation, left to right: Br Fabian, Mick Donnellan, Ger Noonan, Noel Drumgoole, Seán Buckley, Denis 'Big Bird' Lenihan, myself, Paddy McDonnell (masseur), John Corcoran and Paddy O'Sullivan (selector)*

**SNOW PATROL:** *With the Nemo squad before the 1979 All-Ireland club final victory over Scotstown. Back row, left to right: Charlie Murphy, Kieran Brady, Seán Martin, myself, Denis Lenihan, Freddy Stone, Seán Hayes, Mick Kennealy, Jimmy Barrett. Middle row: Frank Cogan, Kieran Collins, Tim Dalton, Colm Murphy, Dinny Allen, Brian Murphy, Jimmy Kerrigan, Denis O'Driscoll and Noel Morgan. Front row: Kieran Murphy, Jerry Weldon, Tom Hennebery and Leonard O'Keefe*

**PROMISED LAND:** *Celebrating the 2003 All-Ireland club final victory with my great friend Jim Cremin*

**CLUB v COUNTY:** *Even when I was training Cork, I always remained involved with Nemo at some level. I saw it as a payback for what the club did for me*

# 'I DROPPED TO MY KNEES AND SAID, "THAT'S IT. YOU'VE WON YOUR ALL-IRELAND MEDAL." ABSOLUTE EUPHORIA'

**TWO TRIBES:** *Shaking hands with Galway captain Liam Sammon before the 1973 All-Ireland final*

**THE MEN BEHIND MAGUIRE:** *The Cork side who won the 1973 All-Ireland. Back row, left to right: Donie O'Donovan, team coach, Denis Long, Ray Cummins, Jimmy Barry Murphy, John Coleman, Dave McCarthy, Declan Barron, Ned Kirby and Denis Coughlan. Front row: Jim Barrett, Con Hartnett, Kevin Jer O'Sullivan, myself, Frank Cogan, Brian Murphy and Humphrey Kelleher*

**IT'S OURS:** *Collecting the Sam Maguire with Denis Coughlan and Jimmy Barry Murphy after captaining Cork to our first All-Ireland football triumph in 28 years. I didn't prepare a speech as I thought it would be unlucky*

**TAKING THE MIC:** *Making a speech at a reception the day after the 1973 All-Ireland final as Galway captain Liam Sammon and commentator Micheál O'Hehir look on*

**SISTER ACT:** *My wife Mary with Bernadette (wife of Ray Cummins) and Anne (wife of Frank Cogan) admiring Sam in 1973*

# 'I WAS EMOTIONAL AS I WALKED OFF THE PITCH FOR THE LAST TIME, BUT I KEPT IT QUIET, THE WAY I WANTED IT'

**THREE STRIPES AND YOU'RE OUT:** *Wearing the infamous three-stripe Adidas jerseys in the 1976 Munster final replay against Kerry. GAA rules dictated we were supposed to wear Irish-made gear on the pitch*

**INCOMING:** *Clashing with Eoin 'The Bomber' Liston in the 1981 Munster final. It was accidental but I t*

**EYES ON THE BALL:** *Making a point-blank save from Kerry's DJ Crowley in the 1967 Munster final. It was one of my best games for Cork*

*ith concussion, 11 stitches and a broken collarbone. I spent three days recovering in hospital*

**HAND OVER FIST:** *I clashed with Mick O'Dwyer many times, but we remain friends. This photo was taken after the drawn 1987 Munster final. 'Ye're haunted,' I told him. 'We'll beat ye the next day,' he replied*

**ON THE BRINK:** *Celebrating the 1988 All-Ireland semi-final win over Monaghan. Back row, left to right: Michael Maguire, Jimmy Kerrigan, Danny Culloty and John O'Driscoll. Front row: Frank Murphy, Seán Murphy, myself and Dr Con Murphy. Meath beat us after a controversial final replay*

**WITH A REBEL YELL:** *Celebrating with selectors Dave Loughman and Seán Murphy after the 1990 win*

**PLAY IT AGAIN, SAM:** *The Cork team that beat Meath to retain the All-Ireland championship in 1990. Back row, left to right: Michael Slocum, Teddy McCarthy, Barry Coffey, Danny Culloty, Shay Fahy, John Kerins, Conor Counihan and Colm O'Neill. Front row: Paul McGrath, Stephen O'Brien, Niall Cahalane, Larry Tompkins, Dave Barry, Tony Nation and Michael McCarthy*

**CORKER OF A TIME** — 'I'M PROUD OF MY ACHIEVEMENTS BUT I'M NOT PERFECT. I'D SAY MY TEMPER IS MY ACHILLES HEEL. I WISH I WAS COOLER'

**PASSION PLAY:** *I can hardly contain my joy as the 2006 Munster final replay victory over Kerry unfolds*

**TROUBLE BREWING:** *Tensions rise on the sideline during the 2007 Munster championship defeat to Kerry*

**SILVER LINING:** *With the Philips Manager of the Month award I won after guiding Nemo to All-Ireland success in March 2003*

**THIS IS THE END, MY FRIEND:** *I told Ger O'Sullivan during a training camp in La Manga in early 2007 that I was going to retire that year. 'Not a word,' I said*

**ALLEN KEY:** *With my wife Mary before the 1973 All-Ireland final*

**RISING SONS:** *With Mary, Alan, Brian and Rosie the dog on the eve of the 1990 All-Ireland final*

**HATS OFF:** *I married Mary on the 15th of April, 1971, in the Honan Chapel in UCC. The reception was held in Acton's Hotel, Kinsale*

**DADDY COOL:** *Brian and Mary share Rebel joy after winning the 1994 Munster semi-final against Kerry, while (inset) Alan celebrates the 1989 Munster final victory over the same opponents*

**I'VE FELT BETTER:** *Frank Cogan and John O'Halloran keep me upright during the 1965 Sigerson celebrations*

**MY CUP RUNNETH OVER:** *My son Brian Morgan and little Mark Cogan use Sam as their Christening cot in 1973 with Mary, myself, Frank Cogan and Anne*

## THE NEXT GENERATION

## ALAN MORGAN: 'I'M GLAD DAD ISN'T INVOLVED... I CAN WATCH THE MATCH WITHOUT MY STOMACH CHURNING!'

**FATHER AND SONS:** *Celebrating Brian's wedding to the lovely Aisling with Alan and Mary*

**REBELS UNITED:** *With Dinny Allen, John Speight and Noel Healy at a reception for Roy Keane*

**SPECTATOR SPORT:** *Watching Nemo with Charlie McLaughlin and my lifelong friend Eddie Brophy*

**BHOY-HOOD DREAM COME TRUE:** *I finally pulled on the Celtic hoops (front row, extreme left) with, among others, Kilkenny hurling great DJ Carey, former world snooker champion Ken Doherty and Johnny Giles, for a charity game in 2007. In 1969, I nearly signed for the club I supported as a boy*

We took up where we left off and Cork resumed their league campaign with a couple of good wins.

We were due to play Tyrone in Omagh in our last match. Frank Murphy arranged for us to fly to Derry.

We were given a great welcome in the city. John Hume was there to meet us. He is a man I greatly admire and it was such an honour to met him. We were taken on a tour of the Walls of Derry and given a civic reception. Cork were always made very welcome in the north and I knew how much the GAA meant to the nationalist community up there.

We beat Tyrone and played very well.

There was a great atmosphere on the plane on the way home. We were looked after very well. Frank did a lot of good work that year. The pilot stood us a few bottles of champagne and we had a few pints together when we got back to Cork. The lads got on very well together socially. It reminded me of our All-Ireland-winning team in 1973. There was plenty of work to be done, but I knew the team had the potential to win an All-Ireland. The attitude was right and so was the football.

We were now the second division champions and that put us into the quarter-finals of the National League. We drew with Dublin in the quarter-final and we were a bit unlucky not to win it. Barney Rock equalised with just a couple of minutes to go.

That was that as far as I was concerned. It was a draw and there would be a replay.

When I went back into the dressing room, I noticed the selectors were in a huddle in the toilets.

The selectors asked me what I thought about playing extra-time. It was the first I heard about extra-time. I was under the illusion the game would be replayed.

The first thing that went through my head was that Sully's Quay played extra-time in an All-Ireland colleges semi-final when we didn't have to, and subsequently lost. Cork were a young team and another game against top-class, high-profile opposition would do us no harm at all. The replay might even be back in Croke Park and that was always a boost to the players. The more games you played there, the better.

I told the chairman and the selectors that I was against extra-time. I thought we had an option on whether or not to play on. Cork County chairman Con Murphy wanted to play the extra-time. He didn't get his way and a decision was made not to play extra-time.

What happened next was farcical. The ball was thrown in. Dublin won it. Barney Rock soloed down the field and scored the winning goal, but there was no goalkeeper minding the Cork net. In fact, there was no Cork team on the pitch! Cork refused to play extra-time when instructed to do so by the GAA authorities. Dublin won and we were out of the league.

I went up to Meaghers to meet my pals Jimmy Keaveney and Seán Doherty. Seán was a selector for Dublin. I was still annoyed over how things worked out.

'Ye can have it Seán,' I said, 'if that's the way ye want to win it.'

What I didn't realise was that I was in the wrong. The rule stated that Cork had to play the extra-time, but I didn't know that when I was talking to Seán. It had nothing whatsoever to do with Dublin.

There was another rule that mitigated against us in the league. Two of our best players were unable to play for technical reasons. Shea Fahy and Larry Tompkins trained with us all through the league campaign, but we could not play them until their transfers from Kildare were sorted out. Shea had been with the army in Collins Barracks in Cork for about five years prior to joining us.

I first heard about Shea from his army colleague Seamus Coughlan, who of course played with Cork and Nemo. Seamus arranged a meeting for me with Shea in Clancy's Bar in the city centre.

Shea told me he was fed up of travelling up and down to Kildare. It was as simple as that and Shea transferred to Nemo and Cork.

Larry Tompkins was also a Kildare player. Larry was working in New York with the Collins brothers from Castlehaven in West Cork. In fact, the Collins boys played for Donegal in New York with Larry.

Their brother Christy who was a builder arranged a meeting with Larry in Skibbereen Golf Club. The meeting went well. Larry wasn't going to play with Kildare again. He had a falling out with Kildare over his travel expenses from New York. It was agreed he would play club football with Castlehaven, inter-county with Cork and he would work for Christy as a carpenter.

Neither Larry nor Shea was actually born in Kildare. Larry was born in Wicklow and Shea was born in Galway. Both men gave a hundred per cent commitment to Cork.

The pieces were beginning to fall into place.

\* \* \*

We were confident of a good showing in the 1987 championship. There was the acquisition of Shea and Larry, the good showing in the league, and the spirit in the camp could not have been better.

Some of the papers were even talking us up as All-Ireland contenders. We played Limerick in the first round in Páirc Uí Chaoimh on a Saturday night, and we were brutal.

Cork won by four points. We got out of it by the skin of our teeth. Colm O'Neill got a goal near the end to make it comfortable for us.

After that near-miss, we arranged several practice matches in the build-up to the Munster final against Kerry. We played Derry in Parnell Park and beat them by 3-15 to 1-10. I was happy with that performance, and I knew we were there or thereabouts after that.

There was a team meeting on the Thursday night before the Munster final and I went through each of the Kerry players in detail. I always kept diaries in my time as Cork manager. There's a note regarding Ger Power, who of course by then had won eight All-Ireland medals. It went, 'Cannot be underestimated. Intimidation'. The translation is that Power is a real threat and he is well capable of standing up for himself if intimidated.

My take on Mikey Sheehy, who had won his eight All-Ireland, read, 'Nice guy image'. By that I meant don't be fooled into thinking Mikey is a soft touch. Mikey could look after himself when he had to. And he will punish you on the scoreboard.

Basically, I was advocating we should beat Kerry by playing football and not try to rough them out of it, as it would do us no good. Intimidation wouldn't have worked against them.

I think I had Kerry figured out for that Munster final. They were of course All-Ireland champions and were the greatest football team I had ever seen, but I sensed they were on the slide. One thing was for sure – if we played as badly as we did against Limerick, we would be wiped out.

We were very good in the first half of the Munster final which was played in Cork and while we didn't play as well after half-time, we were still the better team. We led by two points going into injury-time. Mikey Sheehy – who else? – played a lovely one-two with Michael McAuliffe to the left of our goal about ten metres out.

Denis Walsh, the current Cork hurling coach, was covering Mikey. I ran over to the back of the goal and I was screaming at our defenders. You were allowed do that in those days. I suppose deep down I wanted to be out there on the pitch with the boys

One of our players came back to help out Denis, who seemed to have Mikey covered. Our player tried to shoulder Mikey but in his enthusiasm he shouldered Denis. I was nearly within touching distance of Mikey. There seemed to be no way Mikey could have scored because there were so many bodies back around our goal. I was even nearer to Mikey when he, incredibly, slid the ball through and into the net. I couldn't believe it. I threw myself face down on the ground in despair.

Fair play to our goalkeeper John Kerins, who took a quick kick-out and by the time I got up on my feet again, we were attacking down the left-hand side. Time was up and we had to score. Christy Ryan pointed, but the ref had already awarded a free. Larry slotted a point. A draw. We showed incredible resolve that day, especially at the end. There's one story that epitomises the spirit that ran through that Cork team.

Niall Cahalane went over on his ankle a few days before the game and damaged ligaments. Dr Con did a great job and gave him a pain-killing injection in his ankle on a table in the dressing room just before the game. We all gathered round the table. It was an instinctive thing and it showed how close we were as a group. Cahalane was very good on Pat Spillane that day.

I was very disappointed immediately after the game. Mick O'Dwyer put out his hand and I shook it. I was so upset over losing the lead in the last minute that I just blurted out, 'Ye're haunted'.

'Alright,' said Micko, 'we'll beat ye the next day anyway'.

The disappointment soon faded away and I told the lads the drawn game proved we were every bit as good as Kerry. 'There's no improvement left in Kerry. There is in us. We have the element of surprise still with us. Everyone is saying we lost our chance.'

And of course I threw in Micko's comment after the game. You use what you can. Our attitude was every bit as good for the replay.

Kerry only scored one point in that first half. Mikey, for once, missed several frees and Power got sent off, but we did play very well. We led by 0-7 to 0-1 at half-time and went on to win by 0-13 to 1-5.

.There were some outstanding displays. John Cleary kicked two superb points from way out near the sideline.

Shea Fahy scored two points and Larry Tompkins was outstanding, as he always was against Kerry.

We went on to play Galway in the All-Ireland semi-final.

I drew on my experience to warn the boys that beating Kerry was only a means to an end. I went back to the All-Ireland semi-final of 1971 when we were beaten by Offaly and the sense of anti-climax Cork experienced going into that game after beating Kerry, who were champions.

We were cruising in the first half of the semi-final. In the second half, Galway came into it more and more and went a point up with very little time left. A Galway defender took a line ball and all he had to do was kick it anywhere and the game was over, but he tried to play it short. We won possession and were given a free over 60 yards from the Galway goal. Larry was told he had to score direct and he did. It was one of the greatest frees I have ever seen. A draw.

We won the replay very comfortably. Jimmy Kerrigan scored his first point of the championship and he was clapped on the back by nearly every player on the team as he ran back into position.

I had one worry going into the final against Meath and that was that we already had achieved a lot for such a young team. I told the players, 'It's an All-Ireland final. Don't be satisfied with what we have done so far. You don't get too many chances of winning All-Irelands and you have to take the chance while it's there in front of you.'

We started off very well. Dr Con was sitting beside me and he said, 'Bill, we'll walk this.' I agreed with him, but then two things happened. One of our forwards had a goal chance and he hesitated as he was unsure whether to shoot or pass to Teddy McCarthy. The Meath full-back Mick Lyons came from nowhere and blocked it down. We would have been out of sight if it had gone in.

From that, Meath came up the field and a mistake from us led to a Colm O'Rourke goal. This was a Meath team that had been around a few years. They had been unlucky against Kerry in an All-Ireland semi-final. Their experience showed and in the finish they won by six points. I looked at the game recently on TG4 and we had a lot of the ball and a lot of chances. We should have been much closer to them on the scoreboard.

We were very disappointed, but the feeling within Cork and outside of it was that we hadn't had a bad year which, funnily enough, was the attitude I was trying to warn against in the build-up to the final.

And of course there was controversy. I was suspended after the All-Ireland over an incident in the second half.

Jimmy Kerrigan was clocked off the ball by a Meath player.

I brought the incident to the attention of the linesman, but no action was taken. He just ran away down the line. Most likely the linesman didn't see the incident. I ran out on to the pitch to look after Jimmy who was down on the ground and I was verbally abusing the Meath player who had struck him. The Meath corner-back Robbie O'Malley, who had nothing to do with the original incident, came from nowhere and for some reason I got it into my head he was going to hit me.

I threw a dig at him, but I missed. Next in was Gerry McEntee and he caught me by the shirt and I caught him by the jersey. There was pushing as we held each other off and the next thing it dawned on me, 'Oh Jesus, I'm out here fighting in the middle of Croke Park in an All-Ireland final.'

There was a banquet on the night of the match and I never showed up. We went straight to Meaghers after the game and by the time we got back out to the Lucan Spa Hotel, the dinner was over. I always hate banquets and hangers-on who know nothing about the game talking s***e after a few drinks.

Somehow I managed to drag out the hearing over the All-Ireland row until after the Cork county final.

We played Skibbereen in the quarter-final and we conceded four goals. The selectors proposed me for goals for the next round against Muskerry. My vote went to young Jerome O'Mahony, who had been in goals up to then, but I was picked. I played well against Muskerry and saved a penalty.

I kept my place for the final against Imokilly, who were county champions. We won and I collected my seventh county medal.

I told Jerome he would be on for the Munster championship and once again called a halt to my Nemo career.

The authorities caught up with me. We dodged a couple of hearings, but I was eventually suspended for four months for the altercation against Meath.

I communicated with the Nemo selectors through the wire fence surrounding the pitch for our next game against Stradbally in the Munster Club Championship. I was prohibited from going on to the pitch under the terms of my suspension. The whole thing was a bit of a joke.

We went on to win the Munster club championship and Jerome was in goal. It was our seventh Munster club title.

# CHAPTER 19

# *Play It Again, Sam*

WE HAD LOST THE ALL-IRELAND AND I KNEW I HAD TO LIFT OUR PLAYERS. WE STILL HADN'T SEEN the best of this Cork team.

I was outside the wire for the first couple of league games in the new season. As Nemo had won the championship, we were once again entitled to a selector. Frank Murphy was the only selector who survived from the previous year. Seán Murphy from Kilmurry came in and he had played with me for Cork. Seán was very much on the same wavelength as I was. Bob Honohan and Pat O'Donovan were also appointed. I was still suspended and could not attend team selection. Nemo's Bernard Harrington, who was a good friend, took my place.

The selectors sat down to pick the team for the league game against Armagh. Bernard Harrington proposed Dinny Allen, who was 35 at the time, but he was still playing great football. This caused a bit of controversy in Cork but I had absolutely no doubt but that he was good enough. I knew too there would be allegations of favouritism. Frank was all against Dinny's selection but Bernard outmanoeuvred him. That was some achievement.

Dinny silenced the critics on his comeback and scored three points from play against Armagh, even though we lost the game.

We had an indifferent league campaign and there was no great hype about us for the championship.

Davy Barry was still playing soccer, but I managed to get him back for the championship. I was getting the team I wanted, at last.

We played Limerick in the first round of the championship down in Askeaton and we got out of it by the skin of our teeth. We were behind for most of the game and we only drew level with about seven minutes to go.

Davy came on and he got us out of trouble. Without him we would have been out of the championship. We were dire.

I never let the players have it after a match and I didn't that day either. There was time enough for that at our next team meeting. When players come in after a match, the adrenalin is still pumping and the best thing to do is let them alone.

I travelled home in the car from Askeaton with my co-selectors Seán Murphy and Pat O'Donovan.

'Lads,' said Seán, 'we're turning right here. If we had lost, it would have been left for Shannon Airport.'

We dealt with the display in the Limerick game and prepared for Kerry in the Munster final by playing numerous challenge matches.

The final took place in early July. It was an absolute cracker of a game. The match was very much in the balance until Dinny got a vital goal. It was pure opportunism and in the end we got home by a single point.

Larry Tompkins had an absolutely outstanding game. We moved him out midfield and he scored three points from play. Dinny and Davy justified their selection on the team. Without Davy, we might have lost to Limerick and Dinny's goal was the difference between us and Kerry. That game was the last dying kick of that great Kerry team. They gave it everything, but in the end it was another veteran, Dinny, who won it for us.

Monaghan were our opponents in the All-Ireland semi-final. I went up to see them play in the Ulster final against Tyrone. I still have the notes I made on that match. The weak links on the team were identified and Gerry McCarville and Nudie Hughes were their stand-out, top-class players.

Michael Maguire came in for John Kerins who was injured and he was excellent. Michael was unlucky in that Kerinsy was around at the same time. Maguire was very reliable and never complained. He was a manager's dream.

We beat Monaghan in the semi. We scored a crucial goal just after half-time when Barry Coffey shouldered one of the Monaghan players as he came out with the ball. Davy finished off the turnover with a goal.

The Monaghan player who was tackled by Barry broke his jaw, but there was nothing malicious in the tackle.

The All-Ireland final was against Meath.

There were the usual practice games, and I felt our lads were ready for a really big performance. Meath were a tough, battle-hardened team but we were the better side on the day.

Steven O'Brien came on to mark Colm O'Rourke, who was causing us serious problems. Steven played a blinder. I knew he would come good. He was an instinctive, natural player and the best way to coach him was not to coach him at all.

The first I heard of him was when I was in America when he won an All-Ireland colleges with Críost Rí. His dad Mick was a good friend. I knew his background and I knew he wouldn't let me down. He was only 18.

Meath scored from the next play after a rare miss from Larry.

Then one of our lads late-tackled a Meath player when we had the ball won. Another point.

Meath got a line ball which should have gone our way. Meath's David Beggy won the ball in front of our goal. He went down very easily, in my opinion, and the referee Tommy Sugrue from Kerry whistled for a free in. In my view, it was one of the softest frees of all time. Meath scored and the ref blew up for a draw. I felt we had been hard done by. No doubt about it.

To my dying day, I can honestly say it definitely wasn't a free. And even when I think about it now, it still cuts me up.

I tried to lift the boys. 'Ye beat 'em once. Ye can do it again. Ye are a much better team. Teams usually lose when they miss chances, but we didn't. That shows how good we are.'

There were some incidents in the drawn game that were referred to in the build-up to the replay. Dinny caught Mick Lyons with an elbow. Barry Coffey went to shoulder O'Rourke and caught him just below the ear. Niall Cahalane was involved in an incident with Brian Stafford and Stafford went down. It wasn't anything premeditated. We just went out to win.

There was a lot of talk in the press that Meath were going to get stuck in. The replay wasn't played until Sunday, the 9th of October, fully three weeks after the drawn game.

Because of all the talk about retribution by Meath, my instructions were, 'If there's a row, the whole team should pile in, not necessarily throwing digs but backing each other up. But throw digs if you have to.'

One of the Meath players hit Cahalane and our fellas, every one of them, were in like sharks. Meath had a player sent off and my instructions were to play football from then on.

In other words, I cancelled the 'one in, all in' plan.

I repeated that message at half-time. 'Lads, I said what happened happened. Play football from now on. No retaliation. No piling in'.

It was the biggest mistake of my footballing life. Meath roughed us up and the boys didn't respond in kind because of my instructions. It was like giving them guns without ammunition.

We were two points up and cruising when a cross-field kick was intercepted and Meath went down to score a point. Meath then hit a purple patch. They scored some fantastic points and went four up. We brought it down to a single point, but time ran out on us.

Fair play to Meath. I take my hat off to them. They were down to 14 men and trailed by two points. You can't take it away from them. Whatever about the drawn game, they were worthy winners this time. That was a good Meath team.

The Meath psyche is a mix of stubbornness and arrogance that makes them so hard to beat. I respect that. We didn't get on too well back then, it was open hostility. And they had the better of us which made it even harder to take.

We had lost two in a row. I was shattered. Still, though, I had an unshakeable belief we would win an All-Ireland. I knew I should have told the boys to retaliate in the drawn game. It still haunts me. Maybe I was too much of a purist at times.

That defeat was very hard to take, but there was always Nemo. Jerome O'Mahony was in goal for the year and even though I was retired, I was still sub-goalie! The Burren from Down knocked us out at the semi-final stage of the All-Ireland club. John Treanor destroyed us the same day. Jerome was injured and I played yet another 'last' game for Nemo in the county semi-final against Glanmire.

I was 43 years of age and I still did the same training as the rest of the lads. Jerome came back for the final. We beat Duhallow and that was our ninth county.

There was another bonus from winning that one. The Cork Board decided the county champions should have the power to nominate all five selectors. The then chairman of Nemo, Paddy Quinn, called me up to a meeting of the club executive.

'Bill,', he said, 'you know we can pick the selectors. Who do you want?' It was typical Nemo. They always gave me fantastic back-up.

This was hugely significant. Just a few years previously I didn't even have a vote at selection. Now I could pick my own selectors.

I decided to go for a fair geographical spread. Cork is a huge county and there's no way you could cover all the games unless you had selectors in every region. Seán Murphy was from Mid-Cork. He was there the previous year and I kept him on. Seán was also assistant trainer and we were very close.

Mick Farr came in from Dunmanway in West Cork and I had great time for him going back to 1976 when he was a selector. Dave Loughman was brought on from East Cork. He was an excellent man to have around the camp.

There was one more and I felt I had to have a County Board man on the selection committee. It was a choice between Frank Murphy and Bob Honohan. It was important to have a board man on the committee from the point of view of communicating our needs. I chose Bob Honohan, because I thought he knew more about football than Frank. Bob knew his way around the County Board and he also represented North Cork.

And of course I represented the city. I was getting my way at last and there would be no excuses this year.

We had a good win over Armagh in the quarter-final of the league and we beat Kerry in the semi by ten points to four. We had Kerry's measure that year.

The final was in Croke Park against the Dubs and we won that one by a few points in what was a very good game. We missed Shea Fahy who was in the Lebanon with the Irish army. Larry and Teddy

McCarthy were midfield. We played Steven O'Brien and Barry Coffey at wing-forward and they were two fierce hard-working wing men. The two lads trailed back whenever they could to act as extra defenders. It seems to me that what we were doing 20 years ago came back into fashion in recent years and was heralded as some sort of brilliant take on GAA tactics.

The reward for winning what was known as the Home Final was a trip to New York to play the locals in the National League final proper over two games on an aggregate basis.

I was of course delighted with the thought of getting back to New York. I told the lads to do their best to put up a good score and then they could enjoy the week between the first and second legs.

We beat New York by seven points which wasn't a huge lead and shows just how high the standard was in New York back in the late eighties.

The lads had a good week of it and they enjoyed themselves, but we trained in Central Park. Teddy McCarthy had gone up to Boston. There was no sign of Teddy on the day of the second game, and I kept on asking, 'Where the f**k is Teddy?'

We got to Gaelic Park and there was still no sign of Teddy and there was another 'where the f**k is Teddy' when we togged off.

We had to pick the team without him. The team were walking around behind the band when someone came up to me and said, 'Billy, Teddy is outside the gate and he's looking for his gear.'

'Tell him he can stay outside the gate.'

We won the match by a goal and the National League with it. Dinny was captain.

Tony Nation was chosen as the Cork captain by Nemo, but he had been dropped and so Dinny lifted the cup. I didn't like having to drop Tony. It wasn't that he was playing badly. It was just that others were playing better. County came before club when I was coaching Cork.

I didn't say too much to Teddy over arriving late for the game. I always believed in giving the players a bit of leeway. They are after all young lads, who are entitled to a social life. There were accusations that I was too close to the players and yes I enjoyed a few drinks with the squad. I was still playing the odd game and was one of the boys. Some managers took a different approach, but that was me.

It was great to win a national title, but there was a downside. Colman Corrigan, our full-back, suffered a serious injury when his Achilles tendon snapped. The injury was to put him out for the rest of the year.

Colman was up there with Humphrey Kelleher as one of the great Cork full-backs. He was probably the best full-back in the country at the time of his injury and aside from that he was a great lad to have around the squad. He was a real leader and always in the thick of the sing-songs.

I called to Colman's house in Macroom and ordered him back to training. I left Colman standing on the doorway and didn't say another word- I didn't want to patronise him. Colman didn't miss a single training session that year, even though he was on crutches for months. The players really responded to that. He lifted all of us.

We were drawn against Tipperary in the first round of the Munster championship.

Neill Creedon from Nemo played full-back and he was a much underrated player. We won well and if we lost Colman, it was balanced out to some extent by the fact Shea Fahy was back from the Lebanon.

Once again, we were up against Kerry in the Munster final and we won by three points. John O'Driscoll scored a great goal in that one. He always had that rare ability to sneak away unnoticed . We were always comfortable, but Kerry scored a goal near the end which left it a bit hairy for the last few minutes. Mick Slocum came on and he was brilliant that day. He cemented his place on the team for the rest of the year.

There was a huge build-up to our semi-final against Dublin. The papers were full of it. Dublin always attracted publicity and when you played against the Dubs, you could be certain of a huge crowd and a brilliant atmosphere.

We played against a gale and desperate rain in the first half. Dublin were buzzing and went into a 1-4 to 0-0 lead.

John Cleary then scored two penalties and we went in a point up at half-time. We were in a very strong position and when Keith Barr was sent off early in the second half, we were looking good. In the end we won by four points.

We met Mayo in the final. I knew if we didn't win this one, it was day-day, bye-bye for me. Cork started brilliantly and we raced into a four-point lead. Willie Joe Padden got their first point and it really lifted them. Mayo scored a goal from nothing in the second half and went into a one-point lead. 'Oh God,' I thought to myself, 'is this happening all over again to us?'

We equalised and Kerinsy made a fantastic fingertip save from Anthony Finnerty. Mick McCarthy came off the bench and he scored three great points from play. Cork were All-Ireland Senior football champions for the first time since 1973.

Dinny lifted the Sam and nothing could have given me greater joy. I felt sorry for my clubmate Tony Nation, but his turn would come. There are times when you have to make tough decisions and it really eats you up.

Dinny said in his victory speech that 'it was Billy Morgan's belief in us that drove us on.' That meant so much to me.

I knew if we had lost, I was gone as manager and that was the way it should be. There was a moment of self-doubt half-way through the second half of the All-Ireland final when Mayo got the goal. I said to myself, 'Are we jinxed or what?' But that didn't last too long. I had faith.

The winning of the All-Ireland justified our leaving for America. Mary stood by me all along and she backed me all the way through. I was convinced that once I took over, Cork would win an All-Ireland. I had put so much into this yet the overriding emotion was one of relief.

\* \* \*

We went home to Cork the next day. The team bus came into the city centre round Barry's Corner. There was even a bigger crowd than in 1973, when I won my All-Ireland as a player.

And, once again, there was no better place to be. It was a kind of Cork heaven. I was lucky to experience it twice up to then. I have to say though, it's better as a player. There's nothing better than playing. I would have loved to have been out on the pitch and maybe that's the reason I spent so much time out there during matches!

Nemo won the All-Ireland club title in March. We beat Clann na nGael of Roscommon in the final. Denis O'Sullivan came out to midfield from full-forward. He was only 19 and he dominated the middle with Steven O'Brien, another 19-year-old. I was still coach.

I was lucky enough to become the first man to train the All-Ireland Senior and the All-Ireland Club champions in the same year.

That was one of the better ones.

# CHAPTER 20

## *'Semtex'*

**THIS WAS THE YEAR I WAS GIVEN A NEW NAME. I WAS CHRISTENED 'SEMTEX' AND THAT WAS** the players' nickname for me from then on. And yes there were a few explosive moments that year.

The big aim for 1990 was the winning of the two-in-a-row and if we could beat Meath in the process it would make the win all the sweeter.

The boys celebrated, but I kept Donie's words in mind. The players didn't socialise as much as we did. They were a good crowd to party, but they did it at the right times. And of course they trained very hard. It wasn't just at the team sessions. Larry was a fitness fanatic and he trained all year round. Most of the lads did a bit on their own. They were a great bunch to be out with. The sing-songs were rousing, especially when Colman Corrigan got going. And I loved their company.

Then again I wasn't a player and wouldn't have been out and about as much. I was captain in 1973 and that meant I had to attend a lot of events. This time around I took it a lot easier.

Castlehaven won the county and they were entitled to a selector for the 1990 championship and league. The custom in Cork was that if you won the All-Ireland, four of the same selectors stayed on. It meant one of us had to go. There was a vote taken at the Board and poor Mick Farr, who was an excellent man, lost out. I was sorry to lose Mick, but I was lucky to get Christy Collins who had introduced me to Larry and we also played together with Cork.

One thing we all agreed on was that the big motivation for the year was to beat Meath. We didn't want it to be said that we had never beaten Meath. There was history there and we craved revenge.

Once Christmas was over, it was back to work. I had no problem with any of the players. They were up for it again. My notes from a team meeting on the 29th of January give a good insight into our mindset.

We went through the advantages and disadvantages of being the All-Ireland champions.

On the one hand, everybody was out to beat us, but then there was the extra confidence, which more than made up for that. We emphasised team loyalty and looking out for one another. I told the lads we would review the panel after the league and there were no guarantees of a place on the team for anyone. I reminded the boys of what had happened to us in 1974 and told them we could become one of the greatest teams of all time. It was all about self-belief and the will to win.

Conor Counihan, even then a leader, spoke at the meeting. He just said it was time to forget about last year and get on with winning the All-Ireland for a second time. And again the big thing was to beat Meath. Kerry weren't even mentioned. Meath were still considered to be the top team in the country.

We played our first league game against Down. It was a disaster. Our flight was cancelled because of fog and we only just made the game in Newry. We were beaten by 2-15 to 1-9. It was the excuse I needed.

My method was to wait until the team meeting on the Wednesday after the game. Players are pumped up in the dressing room after matches and there's always the danger of a blow-up. It's best to wait a few days to give them time to think about the game.

We were a long way from where I wanted us to be. I couldn't go too far this time – we had all been at Barry Coffey's wedding the day before the match! And I celebrated as much as anyone.

I have a note in my diaries of a comment Mary made to the effect that we were going the same way as the 1973 team in that we hadn't really stopped the celebrating. I think her comment was meant as much for me as the lads.

Colman Corrigan was back after his horrific injury and he had to make a huge effort to get fit. It was a great boost to have him with us but the best full-back around never really recovered.

We really knuckled down but you have to allow players a chance to cut loose every now and then. They make so many sacrifices and they are young lads who need a good night out.

We were invited to play Mayo on St Patrick's Day in Brentford's soccer ground in London.

The squad arrived on the Friday and trained that morning. Dinny Allen came with us and he had a pal, Paul Murphy from Turners Cross, who owned a pub. My idea was this was 'this is March and let's have a real blow-out and get back down to training afterwards'. Corrigan got us going with 'Those Were the Days My Friends'. And looking back on it now, they really were. We even beat Mayo the next day in Brentford.

There was an expedition to Ted Riordan's pub in London after the match and we had another big night. I always drank with the players and I suppose I was one of them. It was an allegation that was to be thrown at me a while later by the Cork County Board.

\* \* \*

We were back training the following Wednesday and we qualified for the league quarter-final against Kildare in Portlaoise. I was delayed by fog. This time I was in Birmingham for a Cork function and I only arrived in the dressing room at half-time.

I slagged Cahalane in London as there was some talk he wouldn't be coming with us on the trip.

'Thanks for coming, Niall,' I said sarcastically when Cahalane showed up at the airport.

Then when I made the late entrance in Portlaoise, Cahalane got his own back.

'Thanks for coming, Billy.'

There was a big laugh in the dressing room. I was always slagged by the players when I had it coming and I took it. That was our way of making sure none of us lost the run of ourselves. We won that game by five points and who should we come up against in the semi-final only Meath on the 15th of April.

It was a dirty game. One of the Meath players struck Davy Barry from behind when the play was up at the other end of the field, and he had to go off. He didn't know where he was.

Cahalane and O'Rourke were having a right go at each other, but at least it was man to man. Niall finally got sent off when he blew Colm into an advertising hoarding. Cahalane always gave as good as he got, but Davy never got involved. He was only ever interested in playing football.

We lost the game. I remember distinctly saying in the dressing room after the match, 'Lads, this is the last time we will ever be beaten by Meath physically. Stand up to them. Last year we ended the Dublin bogey. This year we'll do the same to Meath. Be men. Be men.'

The day we lost the National League was the day we won the All-Ireland.

\* \* \*

We were sent to New York and San Francisco along with the All-Stars as a reward for winning the 1989 All-Ireland.

The first game against the All-Stars took place in New York and we lost by a point, but again the trip was very good for morale and it brought the lads even closer together. There's nothing like a few days away to build up friendships and all of that team got on very well together, just as we did back in 1973.

The trip ran nicely into the championship and I felt we were coming into form at just the right time.

We beat Limerick well in the first round on the 27th of May. Corrigan came on for his first championship start since his injury and we looked to Kerry in the Munster final.

There was another weekend away two weeks before the Kerry game.

I allowed the lads a few drinks after we played Mayo and Frank Cogan and myself went back to the team bus, only to discover the players were in a pub across the road. Dr Greg Murphy was our team doctor for the weekend as Dr Con was away. Dr Greg was on the piano when we entered the pub and the place was rocking. I intended to send the lads back to the bus, but the craic was so good we left them there for another couple of hours. And we stayed with them. We arrived in

Carrick-on-Shannon at three in the morning. It was yet another incident that seems to have been part of a County Board investigation in the years that followed.

We only had 16 players for the game against Leitrim. During the game we had an injury. Michael Maguire went out the field and I went in goal. It was my last game for Cork, definitely. It was a great weekend and once again we were very much in the better of it as a squad. By the way, Leitrim beat us by ten points and we made sure word got back to Kerry.

Anthony Davis, Teddy Mac, Barry Coffey, John O'Driscoll and John Cleary were all injured. That was five All-Ireland medallists who weren't involved. Mick O'Dwyer had retired and Kerry were now coached by my old friend from Strawberry Hill, Mickey Ned O'Sullivan.

We honestly didn't know what our team would be until we met up in Jurys on the morning of the match. Colm O'Neill, in particular, didn't know whether he would be picked or not. We played him corner-forward and he scored 11 points for us. Most of the great Kerry team were gone by now and we beat them by a score of 2-23 to 1-11.

Kerry were beaten well before the end and many of their supporters were leaving early. Someone told me after that he heard a Cork supporter shout, 'Lock 'em in and make 'em watch.'

Nemo played UCC in a county championship game just a few weeks before the Munster Final. I went out to talk to Ger O'Regan of Nemo and his marker followed him right over to the sideline. Then I told the UCC lad to 'f**k off outa that' but he refused to budge.

I elbowed him into the chest. The player went down. Someone had a verbal go at me. The game finished up and I was hit by an umbrella as I went into the tunnel. Someone called me a tramp. There was afters in the tunnel, but I didn't physically get involved with anybody.

The matter was on the agenda for the next County Board meeting which was held 'in camera'. Con Murphy, the former president of the GAA stood up to make a statement. I had a 'Deep Throat' at the meeting. Con Murphy's statement was that I was 'a disgrace to my club, my county and my family and that I did not deserve to lead Cork out in the Munster final'.

There was a full County Board investigation. The Board called me in after the Munster final and I was suspended for two months which meant I would miss the All-Ireland semi-final. Now suspension meant different things in different counties. Some counties would have allowed me to continue to train the team, but the situation at that time in Cork was that I wasn't allowed to train Cork.

However, I ran into Denis Conroy, chairman of the County Board, just outside Páirc Uí Chaoimh a few days after the suspension. I was on my way to meet the selectors to discuss who would train the team.

'What's my story?' I asked the chairman.

'How do you mean?' asked Denis.

'Am I going to be allowed to train the team, or what?'

'Listen here, Billy boy. Don't you worry about anything. You leave it all to me. Go away now and train the team. Do what you normally do. I'll stand over you.'

I passed this on to the other selectors at our meeting. Bob Honohan had grave reservations when I told him I had the chairman's backing.

'I'm going to have to tell the Board you're training the team, if I'm asked about it at a meeting'.

There seemed to be no way out. I had to step down and I had it set up that Frank Cogan would train the team. I know the situation would have been different in other counties, but Cork took a very strict view.

Frank was as good a trainer as anyone. I still made out the schedule for the training sessions and I would discuss what we were to do every evening with Frank.

I never missed a training session, even though I wasn't allowed take part. I stood up on the terrace and kicked back any high balls that landed near me. I kept in touch with the players over the phone.

We arranged a Cork A v Cork B game in Skibbereen early in August, just a week before the All-Ireland semi-final. I was on holiday at the time in Goleen, which was just down the road from Skib.

There were still the trips to training on Tuesday and Thursday evenings and I continued my job at the back of the goal, but by now I was getting very frustrated. I had a chat with the selectors just before the game in Skibbereen and then I went up to the bank on the side of the pitch to watch the game with my friends Jimmy Keaveney and Peter Rooney who had come down to West Cork for the week with their families.

'What are you doing coming back up here?' asked a puzzled Keaveney.

'I'm suspended, Jimmy.'

And Keaveney doubled over laughing.

'That's a joke,' he said. 'It couldn't happen anywhere else only in Cork.'

I said to myself the man is right and I went over to the selectors after the game. Christy Collins was chairman and I told him what Keaveney had said. Christy said to leave it with him.

The following Tuesday night we had training in Dunmanway. I moved training to West Cork on Tuesdays to give the local boys a break from the travelling. Bob Honohan was at a County Board meeting on that Tuesday night so I took the training session. I was informed that Bob would not be present at our final team talk in Jurys Hotel on the following Thursday night.

We had a swim and sauna at 7pm. The team meeting was fixed for 8pm and after that we would have our meal. I went in for a swim and sauna as usual. I went up to the team room and got my notes ready and checked out a bit of video we were showing.

We were running a bit late and the meeting did not start until about 8.25pm. I took out my notes and started up the video.

Who walked in only Bob. If the meeting had started on time he would have walked in on the middle of it. I panicked and handed my notes to Frank Cogan, who was sitting beside me.

'You take the meeting Frank,' I said.

'Ah Bill, I can't. I've no glasses. I won't be able to read a word.'

Seán Murphy, who was not only a co-selector, but a close friend, took all the selectors out of the room to discuss the matter.

It appeared that Bob was not pleased with what he saw as a clear infraction of the rules. While the selectors discussed the situation out in the hallway, I took the team meeting.

The following morning I had a phone call from Frank Murphy.

'We have been made aware of the meeting last night,' he said. 'If the County Board receive a complaint, there will probably be a further suspension'. We both knew what that meant. 'Further suspension' meant that I would be out until after the All-Ireland final.

'In the meantime,' continued Frank, 'you must stay away from the team on Sunday.'

I couldn't even go up on the train with the lads. Initially it was agreed that I was to stay in a bed and breakfast near the Burlington Hotel, where the team was overnighting. Eventually, I was given a room in the Burlington, but in a different part of the hotel from the players.

Seán Murphy had brought it up at the meeting that surely I would be allowed to take the team on the morning of the match, but Bob disagreed and stated that would be breaking the rules. Bob said that if he was asked by the Board if I took the meeting he would have to tell the Board, as he could not tell a lie. I was upset over his stance, as the meeting would have been held behind closed doors. Bob's view was that he was obeying the rules of the Association.

I was up in the Hogan Stand for the game. Someone arranged for a walkie-talkie so that I could talk to the lads on the sideline during the match, but it didn't work. I wasn't allowed into the Cork dressing room at half-time.

Dave Loughman and Seán Murphy came down to the back of the Hogan Stand to get my views at half-time. I couldn't go near the players. I felt like a leper especially considering how much I had put into Cork football. The rules were implemented, but other counties took a different view and I felt hard done by. I had put my life into Cork. No one could say they weren't implementing the rules, but there's the human side of it.

Oh and by the way, we beat Roscommon in the All-Ireland semi-final. The players stood by me all along. As usual, we dealt with the problem by slagging.

And that's how I was nicknamed Semtex.

# CHAPTER 21

# *The Year Of The Double*

THE SUSPENSION RAN OUT ABOUT A WEEK AFTER THE SEMI-FINAL AND THERE WAS STILL plenty of time left to prepare the team before the final against Meath.

We wanted to beat Meath more than anything in the world. They had beaten us in two All-Ireland finals and there was a needle that was made even worse by our game against them in the semi-final of the National League.

I still have the detailed notes of the first team meeting when my suspension ran out. I felt it was important to set the tone for the next three weeks of training in the build up to the All-Ireland final.

I told the boys that 'Meath would be hard to beat, but they were beatable.'

The plan was that by the All-Ireland we would be at our peak physically and mentally. The tactical battle would be crucial.

Donegal lost the semi-final to Meath because they held up the ball, and were too slow in delivering it to the inside men. We needed to play at pace. And the big thing was we had to train the way we played.

I kept emphasising the physical side of the game at training. The players were told there should be no mouthing or threats. If they had to hit a fella, they should shut up, hit him and get on with it.

We drilled it into the players that we would have to respect Meath and the way we should respect them was by standing up to them. Cahalane said he would belt any Corkman who stood off a Meath man and he meant it.

The hurlers had won the All-Ireland just three weeks before us. I was sitting up in the Hogan Stand when the final whistle went. A Cork supporter came over to me and said, 'It's up to ye now.'

The last time Cork or any team won the double was a hundred years previously and that was won by club sides representing the county. There was no pressure on us as far as I was concerned. The buzz around the city in the lead-up to the match was incredible and if anything that helped us. I don't really think the double came into it as much as our desire to even things up with Meath.

Our masseur Kid Cronin was a vital part of the set-up and he used his boxing brain to get his views across. 'They are granite-jawed and stubborn. If we can't knock 'em out, we have to outpoint 'em. Be prepared to go the full 15 rounds.'

Even though I had it in for Meath, I did respect them for the men that they were and all that they had achieved, but the overwhelming thought was that we had to do whatever it took to beat them.

We started brilliantly in the final. Colm O'Neill was having a blinder at full-forward and he hit the crossbar early on. We were winning all the battles and then just before half-time, there was an incident that could have changed the game.

Colm had stood up to the teak-tough Meath full-back Mick Lyons who was their father figure and a Meath hero for many years. Normally, Colm was quiet as a mouse. He was a lovely fella who never shirked but didn't get involved in punch-ups either. Colm had the ball in his hands and Mick tried to grab the ball from Colm to take a quick free. Colm hit Mick a belt of a fist right in front of the referee. In fairness to Mick, he didn't go down. He just stood there. I think if Colm was more used to throwing digs, he would have been cuter about it!

Colm was sent off. I think we might have fired him up a bit too much, as that wasn't his normal form at all. The referee didn't really have any choice. Poor Colm was devastated.

We were very, very positive in the dressing room at half-time and we just wanted to go out and win it for Colm's sake. We still believed we had every chance of winning.

Cork went four points up in the second half and every one of our players played magnificently. Paul McGrath and Mick McCarthy were up front on their own and ran all over from left to right and touchline to touchline. Mick did his knee and John O'Driscoll came on to do a big job for us. Paul was exhausted and near the end we brought on John Cleary, who was unlucky not to start. Larry did his cruciate, but he still played on and incredibly kicked over two vital frees after suffering the knee injury.

Shea Fahy and Danny Culloty dominated midfield. Danny had a blinder. Shea was man of the match and deservedly so. He got four points from play.

We didn't stand back from the physical challenges. In fact, we were the aggressors. Barry Coffey buried Liam Hayes with a shoulder tackle. The other wing-back, Mick Slocum, turned to Barry and asked, 'Is he dead?' The two of them were great buddies and they just got a fit of laughing at a vital stage of the game, with just a few minutes to go. Conor Counihan, as always, was totally dependable at centre-back in what was a dominant half-back line.

The defence played as a unit stuck close to their men. Maybe they were more afraid of Cahalane than they were of Meath! The Meath full-forward line of O'Rourke, Stafford and Flynn were up there with the best of them. Steven O'Brien and Niall Cahalane didn't wipe out O'Rourke and Stafford but they managed to keep them from controlling the game. O'Brien was only 19 and he had a good game on Colm. He was mature and nothing fazed him. Steven was one of the best players I have ever seen.

Tony Nation was on Bernard Flynn, who was always dangerous and nearly impossible to mark. Tony had missed out the previous year when he was dropped for the final.

There were calls in the media that he should be dropped again after he had a poor semi-final against Roscommon. One headline read 'A Nation Once Again' when it was announced that he was on the team. That can't have been easy for Tony and his family.

I rang his house a week before the game. His wife Emer answered.

'Sorry Billy, but Tony isn't here.'

'It's not actually Tony I'm looking for, it's you.'

She seemed surprised.

'For the next week Tony is going to need his family around him and you have to be very positive.'

Emer was brilliant and so too were his family. Tony had a great game and silenced his critics. I couldn't have been more delighted for him.

It was the most satisfying day of my coaching career.

Even though we had won the All-Ireland the year before, we could not call ourselves a great team until we beat Meath.

They beat us with 14 men and we beat them with 14 men. It was an absolute pleasure. The slate was wiped clean.

There was the usual parade on the open-topped bus and we got a huge welcome. You could feel the pride. The double meant so much to the Cork supporters and the hurling captain Tomás Mulcahy was there to meet us on the reviewing stand in Patrick Street.

I got off the bus and who should be there right in front of the platform only former GAA president, Con Murphy. I was still seething over my suspension and angry over the way he spoke about me at the County Board meeting after the UCC game.

He offered his hand but I pretended not to see him. I was stopped by Bishop Buckley and pointing towards Con, he said, 'Billy, do you know this man?'

And Con put out his hand again.

I ignored him and moved off saying, 'I'd better go down to the lads.' And I walked away. It was a snub that would have massive consequences for me.

\* \* \*

Nemo were knocked out of the Cork county championship in what was a very controversial match against Duhallow in the semi-final. Frank Murphy was the referee and, in my opinion, he had a very poor game. One of their goals was, as far as I'm concerned, a clear foul but Frank missed it. Dinny thought he should have got a penalty and there was a number of other decisions that went against us.

One of our supporters gave Frank a kick in the shin as he came off the pitch and the Gardaí were called. Our supporter was heard to say afterwards that he didn't kick Frank half hard enough. I wouldn't condone the kick, but we were very frustrated.

# CHAPTER 22

# *Board Games*

**WE WENT INTO 1991 AS DOUBLE ALL-IRELAND CHAMPIONS AND ALL THE TALK WAS OF THE** three-in-a-row.

I was giving serious thought to packing it all in. The win over Meath was the pinnacle of my career as a coach. We had won two All-Irelands on the trot and a National League. No Cork team had ever achieved as much. It takes its toll on you and there's a lot to be said for getting out when you're on top.

I was close enough to quitting, but I bumped into Davy Barry one day in the South Mall and he said, 'Billy, you can't quit now. We're going for the three-in-a-row, boy.'

There were allegations that we had too many city lads, and by implication Nemo lads, on the squad. This upset me greatly. I made it clear from the start that I wanted no city/country divide. I didn't care where the players came from. All I ever wanted was to put out the best 15 for Cork. The players knew that and I never had a complaint from a player that I favoured Nemo.

Dave Loughman lost his place as a selector and he was a huge loss. John Fintan Daly came in as the representative of Duhallow and as the year went on, we got on well.

Danny Culloty was the captain and I had great time for him. He asked me to stay on and I didn't want to let him down either. Little did I think that the small boy I met on that first All-Stars trip over 20 years previously in San Francisco would go on to win two All-Irelands and captain Cork.

There was now an open draw in Munster and we were to play against Kerry in the first round of the Munster championship.

I set out our aims at the very first team meeting in January. We wanted to win three All-Irelands in a row and a fifth Munster title on the trot. The fact the Kerry game was in June rather than July meant we had to get ready earlier.

We had to play Roscommon in the last match of the league and we had to win it to stay in contention. Chris Eubank fought Steve Collins the night before the game and the players went out to watch the fight. I had no problem with that or with them having a few pints.

Frank Cogan and myself stayed in the hotel. We watched the fight in the bar which overlooked the front door. As the night went on it dawned me that I didn't spot any of the players coming in. It was about one o'clock and I was getting more and more annoyed. They were allowed a few pints when they were watching the fight, but they definitely didn't have permission to stay out all night.

Colman Corrigan was one of the first in and I let him have it. His buddy Kerinsy was with him.

Kerinsy said, 'Billy, hold on now a while, you're overreacting.'

'Overreacting! overreacting!' It was said in the high voice that comes out when I'm excited or in a temper. And I ran them up to bed. The rest of the squad got the same medicine. I was hopping with temper.

By the next morning, I had calmed down. I praised Mick McCarthy and John Cleary as they were the only two who I thought hadn't gone out, as I didn't see them coming in. The two lads told me they didn't go out at all. More praise. I was most impressed.

Roscommon beat us by a point. We were out of the league and I wasn't happy. I travelled back down with Barry Coffey and Mick Slocum and I loosened out on the way home. We even had a bit of a laugh about it all. And the lads told me that McCarthy and Cleary were the last two to come home. The night porter told them, 'There's a fella going off his game in there', and he let them in the back door.

I thought it was hilarious. We arranged to stop at Walsh's in Mitchelstown. Mick and John were set up.

The two boys were the last into the pub. They were fierce buddies and they were in great form. Mick bounded in the door. He was an upbeat character, full of fun and always sociable.

I pretended I was annoyed. There was total silence in the pub.

'Did ya go out at all last night, did ya? And ye came home through the kitchen?'

The two boys were stunned.

The rest of the lads gave a huge cheer. And I bought them a pint.

* * *

We played the All-Stars in Toronto on St Patrick's Day in the Skydome. The pitch was Astroturf and it was as big as Croke Park. We realised we had to get our act together and we trained twice at eight in the morning in the Skydome. Cork won the match and we played very well. Sometimes there can be and edge to All-Star games and we stood up to the pressure.

There was the usual weekend away on the June Bank Holiday. That was two weeks before the Kerry game.

We took part in an inter-county tournament that weekend in Castledaly and Roscommon beat us by 5-10 to 2-12. We had a good team out and they shouldn't have beaten us by that much.

We had another match against Offaly on the Monday and we stayed up late the night before. I was with the players and we had a good drink.

Offaly beat us by 4-16 to 0-11. What I didn't know was that there was a record being kept of all these incidents. And remember we were double All-Ireland champions, a feat no team would achieve again for nearly 20 years.

I didn't see any harm in these sessions. We had two weeks to recover. It might appear these Cork players were piss artists. They were anything but. The lads socialised with my okay and then went off all drink in the weeks before the game. You couldn't get a better bunch to train and when they trained there was total honesty with no short cuts. Every player gave his all at every session. I always kept in mind they were only young lads who gave up so much to play football and they were entitled to a social life. In fact, it was part of our success in those years. We were all good friends and enjoyed each other's company.

Liam Hayes wrote that Meath did exactly the same thing and between us we won our fair share of All-Irelands.

Kerry beat us by two points. It came down to a lucky enough goal when a blocked kick screwed over to John Cronin who stuck it in the net brilliantly. We had chances to equalise near the end but Kerry got the last score and won by two points. It was a great game of football and there was nothing in it at the end.

I think our defeat was down to playing four All-Ireland finals in four years as much as anything else. Even though we were a young team, we looked tired.

* * *

Again I was thinking of stepping down.

Our term of office was up, but I didn't think there was any danger of my not being reappointed if I so wished after what was our first defeat in five years against Kerry. And of course we had contested four All-Irelands in a row, winning two of them.

I used to go down Páirc Uí Chaoimh to work out in the gym and one autumn evening I was approached by a well-placed source.

'Billy,' he said, 'there's a move on to get rid of you. There's an executive meeting of the board tonight and they want you out'

It came as a complete shock to me. I can honestly say no one in the Board contacted me or gave me any indication my position was under review until I accidentally ran into my source in Páirc Uí Chaoimh.

I met a prominent Board man as I was leaving the stadium.

'Anything going down?' I asked.

'Ah nothing much, Billy.'

'All's quiet so?' I asked, pretending I hadn't a clue about the move against me.

'Ah yeah Bill.'

'Nothing much happening so?' I wanted to make him suffer.

'Ah no.'

And he couldn't get away fast enough. I knew even by then that the Board man was one of the main movers against me and I took great pleasure in watching him squirm.

Four selectors were nominated that night for approval by the Board and I wasn't one of them. Amazingly, Dave Loughman and Ray Cummins were on the list of proposed selectors. Ray and I were married to sisters. Dave was a friend. They wouldn't have put their names forward if they knew I was to be dropped.

There was uproar at the meeting and there were no selectors picked that night. The recommendation was rejected by 52 to 27.

Another meeting was called a week later and my name was added to the list.

Four selectors were picked: Bob Honohan, Christy Collins, Dave Loughman and Ray Cummins. I was rejected by the majority of the delegates. That was some turn-about in one week. More than likely there was a canvass of delegates in the week between the first and second meeting.

There was uproar in Cork. As far as I was concerned I didn't want to have any more to do with the Board. The incident with former GAA president Con Murphy when I refused to shake his hand didn't help either. I am certain he wasn't in my corner.

It seems someone kept a record of the occasions the players and myself stayed out drinking, even going back to the years we were winning All-Irelands, but from what I can remember no Board member expressed dissatisfaction with our build-up, or with the way I was preparing the team when we were winning.

The players issued a statement to the effect they would refuse to play unless I was reinstated. I had absolutely no part in that, but I was very proud of the way they backed me up. If the players wanted me out, I would be gone without a word. The Beara board from West Cork came behind me 100 per cent and so did several clubs.

The Lord Mayor of Cork Denis Cregan was very critical of the County Board's handling of the matter and questioned why they should sack someone who had won so much. Micheal Martin TD, as he was at the time, came out on my side. Former Taoiseach Jack Lynch called for me to be reinstated. The Evening Echo carried out a poll and 91 per cent of the 3,000 asked came out in my favour. The Board were on the run.

Ray and Dave resigned. They let it be known that, as far as they were concerned, I was treated very badly.

Honohan resigned as a selector. He would not have been one of my supporters. We weren't close. He said he was stepping down in the hope it would 'solve the impasse'. I certainly would not have been prepared to stay on a selection committee with Bob Honohan.

There was only one selector left and that was Christy Collins.

There was a huge outcry around the county.

Frank Murphy called up to my house with the chairman and he asked me to come back.

I made it known I wanted Ray and Dave back in as selectors. Liam Hodnett and Teddy Holland were mooted as their replacements.

I was invited to an informal gathering of a few of the Board members who were on my side and I told them I didn't want to continue on as coach. Every one of them wanted me back. By now, the board were isolated. Public opinion was against them, the players were against them and so too were the majority of Cork footballing people. I told the meeting I didn't want to return without Ray and Dave. The meeting felt Holland and Hodnett were assuming I was happy with them coming in. I wanted Dave and Ray. I had nothing against Hodnett or Holland on a personal basis and the meeting felt that they should be made aware of my position.

Hodnett withdrew when he said he received phone calls putting him under pressure to resign. I issued a statement to the effect I had nothing whatsoever to do with any alleged threatening phone calls. And I didn't. If I had anything to say to anyone, I would have said it to their face.

The players asked me to meet up. We met in Bandon and they asked me to take the job.

I agreed to return solely to back up the players, the Cork supporters and my supporters within the County Board.

Hodnett was replaced by Eamonn Young.

Ray and Dave urged me to take the job. Dave put it well. 'In every war there are casualties and Ray and myself are the casualties. The big thing is we won the war.'

Part of me just wanted to walk away. I decided to get on with the job for the sake of Cork football, but I was deeply hurt by the affair.

The supporters called my name at our first league game against Armagh after I was reinstated. I was embarrassed, but delighted by their support. The right people were still backing me and I was going to make sure I would do everything I could to repay them.

The official reasons for my not being nominated were never given to me and I was never given a chance to respond to the allegations made against me. At the very least the Board should have allowed me to face my accusers like a man – up front and face to face. The meetings were held in camera and the only reports came from leaks to the press. It was the unfairness of the process that really got to me. Surely after my years of service, the very least I was entitled to was to be told what I had done wrong. Natural justice went out the window. Even a criminal is entitled to be told the crimes he is being charged with and will be given an opportunity to respond to those charges.

Mary supported me throughout and she said to the press that I had more to lose than gain by going back 'even though he has already proven himself.'

# CHAPTER 23

# *The One That Got Away*

SOMETIMES YOU JUST NEED TO GET AWAY FROM IT ALL. THE PLAYERS ORGANISED A HOLIDAY in Tenerife in January 1992.

We had a break in the sun in early 1989 and it was a huge help in winning the All-Ireland that year. It really brought us together, focused our minds. By coincidence, Meath were there at the time, and there was hardly any contact other than with Bernard Flynn. I often had a few drinks with Bernard over the years, but there was a cold war in the Canaries. We continued with the sun holidays though. It was the least the players deserved as they couldn't take any break in the summer.

The trip went well and there was the usual build-up for the championship with a mix of National League and challenge games.

After losing to Kerry the year before we had started to rebuild again by bringing in new players. Colin Corkery made his debut and it was obvious from the start he would be a big addition.

Joe Kavanagh came in against Dublin in the last match of the league. He was on the All-Ireland-winning minor team of the year before and he had a great game against the Dubs. He scored 2-3 and it was a case of a star is born. Pat Hegarty, who was another member of the winning minor team, played that day and did well. We won by a point, but we didn't make the play-offs.

Training was going well and we came up against Meath in the Bantry Tournament. We beat them in a very uneventful game for a Cork-Meath clash.

We all met in Jimmy Crowley's Bar at lunchtime the next day. There was a jazz band playing and the singer sang 'Mustang Sally', but he knew only one verse and he asked if anyone knew the whole song.

David Beggy came forward and volunteered to sing the unabridged version. Beggy is a great character and is a fine singer. He brought the house down. We had a special day with Beggy. It was the start of the thaw.

Once again we were drawn against Kerry in the first round of the Munster championship. I know the open draw was good for the other counties and, in fairness, it brought them on a lot, but for me there's only one Munster final and that's Cork versus Kerry.

There was no back-door system back then and if you were beaten in the first round, that was it.

Things started to go wrong on the morning of the match. Larry Tompkins had been training on his own down the Mardyke just a few days before the Kerry game. There was a game taking place on the pitch and Larry took time out to watch it. He took off his socks and he was badly sunburned. To make matters worse, the leg became infected.

We met on the morning of the game, and we weren't sure whether or not Larry could play.

It was decided that morning he couldn't play and we announced the team without him.

Larry came up to me after his warm-up and told me he felt he could play. Mick McCarthy was taken off and Larry was brought on after twenty minutes. It was very unfair on Mick. We missed two penalties and Kerry scored one. Cork lost heavily even though there wasn't very much between us. Our indecision cost us dearly. We should have either left Larry on or off from the start.

This couldn't have come at a worse time. There was all the controversy and now we were knocked out after just one game. There was no way I was going to quit in that way after being beaten so easily by Kerry. I had a two-year term which meant there were no moves against me, that I knew of, in the County Board.

County champions Skibbereen appointed a young fella, Martin Crowley, as their selector and he knew his stuff. Liam Hodnett and Teddy Holland were reappointed and Christy Collins was also with us.

We were definitely better organised for the beginning of the league. The rest did us no harm. I felt rejuvenated after the break.

We were very good against Cavan in the first round of the league and I had a good feeling about the year.

Mark Farr was introduced for the next round. Bit by bit, we were building a new team.

We beat Carlow by 2-16 to 0-0. Ciaran O'Sullivan played in that one. He was to prove to be one of the stars of the team. We were professional that day and while you had to feel sympathy for Carlow, players were playing for their places and it showed. The infusion of new blood was just what we needed.

Larry was still injured and he hadn't played any games for us. There was intense speculation he was rejoining Kildare. Mick O'Dwyer was now the Kildare manager and he made no secret of the fact that he wanted Larry. We were beaten by Kildare in the league and Larry wasn't playing for us which led to even more talk about him going back to Kildare.

We still had six players from the two-in-a-row team, and the new players were blending in well.

I was optimistic about 1993.

I suggested we try Ciaran O'Sullivan at wing-back after I watched him play there for just a few minutes in the position during a practice match. It was one of our smarter moves and Ciaran proved to be the best wing half-back in the country in 1993.

We beat Leitrim in the first league game of the year and drew with Clare, who were, of course, the Munster champions. Don Davis was starting to come through in that team and Bob Honohan's son Liam was also making an impact around centrefield. I never had any problems with Liam. I pulled him aside and told him that any differences between his father and myself were ours and ours alone. And I told him I would always treat him fairly.

Podsey O' Mahoney was another fine player and he made his debut for us against Donegal in the league.

We didn't qualify for the league play-offs. We concentrated on preparing for Clare who had their best ever team. It was a tough draw. Clare were Munster champions and acquitted themselves very well in the All-Ireland semi- final against Dublin. They also had the benefit of a good run in the league. The Banner were managed by John Maughan, who made a huge impact in his first year in charge. For the first time ever, we were the underdogs against Clare.

We kept the boys interested by playing plenty of games. That was the quickest way of building a new team and it seemed to work for us. Mickey Harte has been very successful with Tyrone in not playing challenge matches. My view was that the more matches the better and I never believed in stopping players from lining out with their clubs.

We beat Offaly well in the Bantry Tournament and Mark O'Connor was now beginning to establish himself as a fine full-back. That was a big plus for us. Full-back is a problem position for almost every team and Mark was getting better with every game.

By now we had a settled team.

Larry, though, picked up another injury and he was out for the first-round game in Ennis. We played exceptionally well that day.

Colin Corkery had an outstanding match. He rounded his marker at a vital stage and stuck the ball in the back of the net with absolute assurance. Liam Honohan came on as a sub and he was very effective with Danny Culloty in the middle of the field. Joe Kavanagh scored three points and Ciaran O'Sullivan was brilliant as a converted wing-back. Steven O'Brien made a crucial block-down. My notes from the time summed up the way we played: 'Simple, direct, concentrating and disciplined'. That was my football philososphy.

That was only the first game of the championship and we had to play Kerry in the Munster semi-final.

Larry was back from injury and that was a massive boost, as he always played well against Kerry.

Ireland beat England in the Five Nations that year and we used the game to get lads up for the Kerry match. We quoted Tony Ward who summed Ireland up in a word: 'Hunger'. We showed a video of the Irish winger Simon Geoghegan and his fierce commitment to the tackle. Paul Wallace got the Irish crowd going and we made sure our lads would play the crowd.

We beat Kerry by 1-10 to 0-10.

By now, Larry was an experienced player and very much a team man. In his early days, he tended to try to do too much on his own but now that he was getting older, he was bringing other players into the game. He gave a brilliant pass to Colin who knocked it down to Joe Kavanagh. Joe slotted it past the Kerry 'keeper Peter O'Leary, who had been brilliant against us all day.

Steven gave another mature display at centre-back. I knew we had big players in key positions and that we were capable of winning the All-Ireland again.

You need luck to win All-Irelands and you need to be lucky with injuries. Larry did his cruciate in a club game. I was sick when I heard the news. We needed him more than any other player in the squad. There are always one or two players you just cannot replace and he was one of those.

Brian Corcoran, an excellent hurler, came into the team. I had a job getting him to play. I got him to meet Jimmy Barry Murphy and Ray Cummins who were of course two of Cork's best dual players. I asked the lads to tell Brian of their experiences as dual players and to be absolutely straight up with him, as I knew they would be.

Brian came into the team for the Munster final against Tipperary in place of Niall Cahalane, who was injured.

We raced into an eight-point lead. The one thing you have to watch against underdogs is to give them no chance to get into the game. Mick McCarthy proved his worth with 1-2 and Colin Corkery scored eight points. Mick McCarthy was captain. Mick stayed with me in New York when he played with Leitrim and I was delighted to see him lift the cup. I had great time for him, both on and off the pitch.

Mark Farr was dropped for the semi-final. He had a tough enough time of it against Davy Ryan in the Munster final. Looking back on it now, that was a mistake. Cahalane, who was an automatic selection, came back in and Corcoran held his place.

Brian Corcoran should probably have been given more time to mature as a player. He would of course later grow into a fine footballer and there are few Corkmen who have made such a magnificent contribution to both hurling and football. You could play him anywhere, in both codes, but I didn't do him any favours by bringing him on so soon.

We hammered Mayo, who were now trained by Jack O' Shea, in the All-Ireland semi-final. Derry shocked Dublin in the other semi-final. We were back in the final.

\* \* \*

Back in 1992, I brought in Tom Ryan as a sports psychologist. Tom was a classmate in Críost Rí and he introduced us to his colleague George Tracey.

I read Bryan Robson and Gordon Strachan's autobiographies and they both emphasised that preparation of the head was every bit as important as the body.

George stayed on with us in 1993. He was a very good hockey player and he knew what made players tick. I know he helped several of the lads and it was their choice whether or not they wanted to see him. I think I was probably the first GAA manager to bring in a sports psychologist and George was a big success. He helped us with relaxation in the build-up to the final and I often consulted with him when I was trying to figure out what to say to the players.

That Cork team started the All-Ireland final like winners and we led by 1-4 to 0-1. The football was exceptional and were steamrolling Derry when the game had to be stopped.

There was the usual GAA overcrowding mess and the officials were forced to open the gate at the Canal End, which was the goal we were playing into in the first half. The fans came on to the grass areas all around the goal and the sidelines. The crowd were right down on top of the players. The game was stopped for several minutes and it halted our momentum. Derry had a chance to regroup and they came back into it.

But there was worse to come. Anthony Davis went in to shoulder a Derry player. The Derry player ducked at the last minute and Anthony caught him high. The Derry manager Eamonn Coleman ran on to look after his player and called for Anthony to be sent off. Just before that incident, Cahalane tackled Enda Gormley and it was off the ball.

I wouldn't mind but Cahalane had Gormley in his pocket. In fairness to Cahalane, he had shipped a few very hard tackles before that. Maybe subconsciously, ref Tommy Howard had the Cahalane incident in the back of his mind when he sent Anthony off. Who knows? There was no bias or anything, but in my opinion it was a wrong decision.

We gave away some soft scores before half-time due to sloppy passing and Derry went in two points up. Anthony, just like Colm O'Neill a few years previously, was in a bad way at half-time. We all felt he was hard done by and we came out full of fight for the second half. We started Teddy McCarthy at midfield and Danny Culloty came on for him at half-time. Danny seemed to gel better with Shea Fahy. We should probably have made a change on Joe Brolly as well.

John O'Driscoll scored a great goal to put us a point up and Derry were all over the place, but we couldn't manage to tack on an extra score. There were a couple of refereeing decisions that went against us late in the game also.

Steven O'Brien was going for goal when the referee called him back for a free to us. He should have given Steven the advantage.

Joe Kavanagh had a 14-yard free blocked down from only eight yards away. I couldn't believe it when the ref waved play on.

Derry, to their credit, got the vital scores near the end, but for us it was definitely a case of the one that got away. Derry were a very good team, but I felt we were that bit better. It was heartbreaking. The dressing room was like a morgue. There's no worse place. I felt for the players and it cut me up to see them so down.

\* \* \*

I made up my mind I was going to pack it in and I told Frank Murphy of my decision coming down on the train.

'Hold on a while, Billy,' he said, 'and don't make any rash decisions. Take your time.'

I took his advice and bided my time, but at that stage I had no intention of continuing. I was still playing junior football for Nemo and my links with the club were as strong as ever.

Nemo won the county again and Steven O'Brien was due to be captain the following year. I had great time for Steven, and I felt I should stay on for one more year.

There was a reception for us in the Beamish Brewery in Cork city on the Tuesday after the game. Normally, the Kid Cronin would be the first one there. He loved that sort of thing and he would be doing his best to cheer us all up. There was no sign of him at the reception. The Kid was found dead in bed that morning. The All-Ireland didn't seem as important after that.

\* \* \*

GAA people have to work for a living and I stuck at the teaching. I ran into an old friend Jim Mulcahy back in the late eighties and we got to talking about the Bomber Liston who had packed in teaching and went to work for the Irish Nationwide Building Society in Tralee.

'I don't suppose you'd be interested in a job like that.'

'I might be.'

'I might be able to put a job like that in your way.'

Six months later, Jim called me and told me Sun Life of Canada were opening up an office in Cork.

I took up a job with Sun Life in January 1989 as a sales rep selling life and pension products. I still held on to my teaching job and took leave of absence.

I didn't return to teaching when the first year was up and the new job went pretty well.

In 1990, I joined Eagle Star as a tied agent which meant I could only sell Eagle Star products. I was effectively working for myself and wasn't paid a basic salary. I was dependent on commission and it went very well. There is no doubt that my GAA background and contacts were a huge help in my new career.

I spent three years as a tied agent and in 1993 I was taken on as a full-time employee by Eagle Star. I was in direct sales. We might have been an amateur organisation, but the GAA looks after its own when it comes to business. My GAA background opened doors and while you might not know most of the people you were dealing with, they felt they knew you. I enjoyed the freedom from school as I was out on the road quite a bit and you could always manage to squeeze in a coffee with old friends.

In 1994, I went to work for O'Mahony Walshe who were brokers and that effectively meant I could sell any product I wanted.

By then, I had decided to give up teaching for good. My five years' leave of absence was about to expire and the teachers I spoke to told me teaching had changed quite a bit since I had last set foot in a classroom.

One colleague told me, 'Billy, you have to be so careful about what you say and do. Every word has to be measured.'

I decided I couldn't handle that. I never had any real regrets about leaving teaching, although I sometimes get a hankering for New York in June, July and August.

# CHAPTER 24

## *The Kerry-free Zone*

**WE HAD THE SAME SELECTORS FOR 1994, SO AT LEAST I KNEW WHAT I WAS DEALING WITH.** I worked very well with Christy Collins and Martin Crowley in particular.

We trained differently that year with more emphasis on stamina. There were far more sessions before and immediately after Christmas. We usually followed three-and-a-half-mile runs with a weights session. I did most of the running sessions with the lads and I wasn't last either.

And of course I played yet another last match for Cork against our Under-21s that April when we were short players for a challenge and I didn't let in any goals. There were a couple of tournament games and we introduced Ken Hendricks for a match against Roscommon up in Wicklow. Ken did well and he was a good lad. He was tragically killed in an accident just a few weeks after making his Cork debut.

I brought Conor Counihan in as assistant trainer as he had retired the year before. And we organised a talk from a nutritionist which I think might also have been a first for a GAA team.

We probably trained harder that year and we were in good condition for the first round of the Munster Championship against Waterford. Larry worked very hard to come back and he played his first game in early June, almost a year after he was injured. He wasn't the same player after the injury. Larry never really recovered, but he was still a good player.

We beat Waterford handy enough and picked Larry for the Munster semi against Kerry.

\* \* \*

I was busy outside of football. We opened Billy Morgan's Bar in Marlboro Street in the Cork city centre. Larry owned Handlebars near the Railway Station and he had had enough of the bar business at that time and packed it in. In fact, I advised Larry to open the bar.

I always thought there might be an opening for a GAA pub in Cork and now that I wouldn't be interfering with Larry's trade, I decided to have a go. The plan was that I would keep my job and Mary would run the bar. On our first night the place was packed and Ireland beat Italy in the World Cup, but I was more worried about Kerry.

That Munster semi was one of Cork's greatest wins.

Cork came from five points down playing against the wind with only 15 minutes to go. We clawed our way back into it. Teddy Mac came on and scored two points. Steven took on the whole of Kerry. He brought us level with a great goal and we won by two points in the end.

The game was also memorable for another reason. There was an incident near the Blackrock end when Colin was tackled and just kept the ball from going out over the line. The linesman gave a lineball to Kerry and I shouted, 'The ball was never over the line'. Kerry selector and All-Ireland medal winner Johnny Mulvihill came from nowhere and had a go at me. 'Shut up Billy you are always trying to intimidate linesmen.' He got me going.

'I'm not trying to intimidate him,' I said. 'I'm only telling him the ball wasn't over the line.'

And we continued in that vein. It got hot and heavy. We squared up but there was no blow struck. Ogie Moran was the Kerry manager and he didn't get involved.

But there was fall out later on that night. I had a good few drinks after the game and finished up drinking with a group of Kerrymen in the pub. Robbie O'Dwyer, Micko's son, and John Cronin, who scored the goal against us in 1991, and Patcheen O'Sullivan were in the company.

I was just about to go to out to Nemo when Dr Con came down and told me Johnny Mulvihill, Ogie Moran and the Bomber Liston were in the bar.

'Okay,' I said to Dr Con, 'I'll go down to see them.'

I think I probably intended to buy them a pint but then I spotted

Johnny Mulvihill and The Bomber. The fuse went. As I passed by, I said, 'Johnny, what the f\*\*k were you up to today?'

Johnny said something back and we started to argue again. The Bomber stuck himself in between us and said, 'Ah now lads. Come on. Take it handy.'

'What are you up to?' I said to the Bomber. 'F\*\*k you. You tried to kill me in '81.'

This was a reference to clash between the Bomber and myself in the Munster final when I was carted off with concussion and a broken collarbone. I hadn't even spotted Ogie Moran at that stage but I was told afterwards he was in the pub.

I turned back to the Bomber, who wasn't even on the sideline when the incident took place, and said, 'F\*\*k off outa here; ye'll get no more drink.'

I then went off out to Nemo. The following day I got a phone call from Dr Con. 'What are you after doing?' he asked. I had forgotten about the event until Dr Con reminded me. The next thing was I had a call from a newspaper enquiring about the incident.

'There's nothing to tell,' I replied. 'It was just a few words in a bar.' I should have kept my mouth shut. The story was on the front page of The Kerryman that following Thursday and from there every paper in the country followed up on it.

I always got well with Kerry people. I knew Johnny Mulvihill from his UCC days and we laughed the whole thing off a few months later in Dublin on the night of the All-Ireland final when we ran into each other in the residents' lounge of The Burlington. We spent the rest of the night in each other's company and are still good friends.

There was fierce slagging in the pub with remarks like, 'This is a Kerry-free zone.'

I have to put my hands up and say I was completely out of order. The Bomber's tackle was accidental and even though we crossed paths a couple of times over the years, I didn't get an opportunity to apologise to him personally for the barring.

There was a breakfast reception in Páirc Uí Chaoimh before the 1999 Munster final and 'The Bomber' was there. I made up my mind to go over and apologise to him, but he was gone out by the time I got to where he was. Cork won the game and I was coming out of the stand after the match when I bumped into 'The Bomber'. This time I was worried he might think I was just coming over because Cork had won the game.

I put out my hand and said, 'Bomber, this is ridiculous that we're not talking after all these years.'

I admitted I was wrong and we shook on it.

I walked down along the stands and I bumped into Ogie and I shook hands with him too.

Later on, in 2008, I met up with the lads at a charity event in La Manga which was organised by Bernard Flynn. We were in each other's company a fair bit on that trip and we got on very well.

* * *

There was never a year that Cork didn't train hard and 1994 was no exception. We were up against Tipp in the Munster final and we gave them every respect. Tipp got an injunction stopping the GAA from suspending Derry Foley just a few days before the game. This was a first and Tipp really put it up to us.

Larry was picked. He hadn't been at all the training sessions and preferred to work out on his own. It didn't bother me that much as I knew he wasn't dodging. Still it would have been better if he trained with us. Looking back on it, I probably let him off a bit lightly, but he was an experienced player who knew his own body.

He scored a point and Colin shot the lights out. That win over Tipperary was hard-earned and it put us into the All-Ireland semi-final against Down.

This was a tough draw. Down had won the All-Ireland in 1991 and they still had most of that team. Again we prepared with several practice games and I felt we were very fit.

We played Down on the 14th of August. The game was even enough until Danny Culloty and Tony Davis had a terrible collision. Danny was carted off but Tony managed to come back on even though he had to be bandaged and stitched. Down scored an early goal and we were always playing catch-up. They beat us by a few points and we had no complaints.

That Down team went on to win the All-Ireland. Ross Carr, DJ Kane, Ambrose Rogers, Paddy O'Rourke and James McCartan were as good as I ever had to face.

It wasn't a bad display from us. We had young players coming through. Cork had won two minor All-Irelands and won the Under-21 championship that year.

We trained a fair bit that October. Teams were training harder and starting earlier. It was now becoming a 12-month game and I felt we had to keep up. There were training sessions right up to Christmas. Mostly we concentrated on three-and-a-half-mile runs with weight sessions afterwards.

We were back training on the third of January and I finished well up in the three-and-a-half-mile run. I always enjoyed running and I still do. I go for a run every Sunday morning and at least twice during the week.

The league campaign was only a means to and end. We trained very hard all through it.

John Kerins had retired at the end of 1994 and was replaced by Kevin O'Dwyer, who waited patiently for his chance. Kerins gave tremendous service to Cork over the years and was up there with the very best in Ireland.

We beat Clare in the semi and Kerry in the final. We played very well and managed to get home by three points in an excellent game. That made it seven out of nine wins for me as a manager against Kerry. The All-Ireland semi-final was against Dublin and there was a massive build-up. The fact that Dublin were in the semi meant there was ten times the usual publicity.

We led by five points after 15 minutes when this young lad by the name of Jason Sherlock scored a goal into the Canal End. Mark O'Connor, his marker, slipped on the tricky surface and Jayo became a superstar that year. We won the next ball from the kick-out but kicked it wide. You always want to score a point straight after the other team get a goal. It transpired that Podsie O'Mahony was fouled as he kicked that one. The ref didn't spot it and neither did I.

Podsie was taken off and I still regret that decision. He was a player I always had great regard for and looking back on it now I felt we acted too hastily. That call still annoys me to this day. That's the thing about being a selector. We make some good decisions but sometimes we get it wrong and that was one of those days.

Jayo's goal lifted Dublin and the momentum carried them through to the final and All-Ireland glory.

\* \* \*

I definitely felt this was my time to go. My two-year term was up and that was that as far as I was concerned. Christy Cooney, the current president of the GAA, was chairman of the County Board and I wouldn't even look at him, never mind speak to him.

Christy was on the executive of the Board when I was shafted and apart from Dan Hoare, who backed me, I never had anything to with any of them after that.

Frank Murphy asked me to talk to Christy and I refused to speak to him. Frank did me a turn and as a favour to him I decided to meet with Christy in Frank's office in Páirc Uí Chaoimh. I told him my grievances and while the conversation must remain private, Christy did say he had regrets about the way my case had been handled. We got on very well after that and I found him to be a fair man.

Christy wanted me to continue. He wanted to change the selection system. Christy's plan was for three selectors. I was to be a selector and coach. The county champions would have a representative and the County Board would appoint the third selector.

I was in two minds whether to go or stay on as manager. Our first league game was against Cavan in Breffni Park. Christy came into the dressing room after the match.'I have a very good selector for you.'

He appointed Paddy Sheehan from Mallow and I took Christy at his word. Bantry won the county and as I had so many friends in the town, I was happy they would pick someone I would get on with. Bantry appointed Terry O'Neill and I decided to give it another two years.

I appointed Colman Corrigan as assistant trainer. We were good friends and he was and is a very good judge of football. Conor Counihan stepped down as he was training his club Aghada.

The fact we had only three selectors meant a lot more work, but Colman was very good with the players. It was another new start.

# CHAPTER 25

## *Out On My Own*

**THE TEAM HOLIDAY HAD BECOME AN ANNUAL RITUAL BY NOW, SOMETHING WE REALLY** looked forward to as a way of kick-starting the new season. In January of '96, we were back in the Canaries for what one Kerry mentor called 'bondage'. Of course he meant bonding.

The 'punishment' – if you could call it that – seemed to work for us. We won the McGrath Cup and qualified for the closing stages of the league. Colin Corkery was clocking up huge scores in almost every game, but Damien O'Neill, who had been playing very well for us at midfield, pulled his hamstring and it more or less troubled him for the rest of the year. He was a massive loss.

In Munster, we were lucky to beat Clare after a replay and extra-time. John O'Keeffe was the Clare trainer by now and we always got on well but I was to meet my good friend Páidí Ó Sé in the Munster final. We kept in touch over the years and Páidí called in to see me in the pub whenever he got the chance. Of course, I returned the favour and called to see him in Ventry from time to time and he was as good as a tonic.

He called into our pub immediately after we beat them in the league quarter-final. Seamus MacGearailt, who was a Kerry selector that year, was with him. And of course Páidí couldn't resist a ball-hop.

'Billy, we said we'd call early.' This was a clear reference to the barring of Ogie, Johnny and The Bomber. I could never get annoyed with Páidí.

One another occasion, he told me of his ambition to manage Kerry. I remember his exact words.

'Billy, the next time Kerry beat Cork, I'll be training them and I'll have them wired to the moon.' He really wanted that Kerry job. I knew his team would have fire in their bellies. Páidí would make sure of that.

Maurice Fitzgerald and Seamus Moynihan changed the course of the Munster final. Moynihan went to centre-back and Maurice Fitzgerald was moved to midfield. Maurice kicked two long-distance frees and Moynihan was excellent at centre-back. A chance injury led to the moves that changed the game, and but for that I felt we might have won. Killian Burns came up from the defence to finish us off.

Kerry had their revenge. Páidí was right!

* * *

I had another year to go but I really wanted out. I felt by now I was too familiar with the players.

I was there too long. There was no doubt but that I was getting tired. Christy said he wanted me to stay, but I told him I would like to see Larry appointed as coach. Larry always trained hard and he drove the lads on at training.

I persuaded Larry to take over and my term as Cork coach was over. There were some good young lads coming through. They had won minor and Under-21 All-Irelands. I had just become too friendly with them and I didn't have the necessary ruthlessness anymore. The last thing I wanted was to hold Cork back.

I intended to take a break from football, but just at that time Dinny Allen stepped down from training Nemo. Dinny had managed Nemo to an All-Ireland club title and he was an excellent coach.

Nemo had been knocked out of the county by a single point for three years in a row.

I was asked to take over. I couldn't refuse. But we had a disastrous year. We were beaten by Bantry in the first round of the county. We were held up in traffic and we only arrived when Bantry were going out on the pitch. Damien O'Neill was on fire but the player I tipped to be as good as any who played for Cork did his cruciate in that game. We were beaten by a point and once again a crucial decision went against us.

Jim Cremin was my right-hand man in Nemo. He played with the Cork minor hurlers in 1969 and won a Harty with Coláiste Chríost

Rí. He was a fierce Nemo man and was with me almost from the beginning as a kind of unofficial sports psychologist. Jim was absolutely brilliant with the players. I thought seriously about bringing him in with Cork but didn't want to have Cork too top-heavy with Nemo men. Once I went back to Nemo, he came on board and he was always a very close ally of my mine.

We did go on to win the Kelleher Shield and at least we won something.

It wasn't all bad news that year.

Brian, Alan and myself also played together on the same team in the City Division junior football league and we won it out.

Georgie Allen coached Sully's Quay when we won the Harty Cup and he was now the president of Nemo. Georgie deliberately held back the presentation of our junior medals at a club function and called the three of us up together. It was a proud moment.

\* \* \*

Away from sport, I went out on my own later on in the year and formed Billy Morgan Financial Services. I was very happy where I was but I always wanted to open my own business. There just wasn't time up to do that with the commitment to the Cork job.

Mary ran the bar but I went in every Saturday morning for a cup of coffee with my pals and we had a good laugh. Sometimes I would go in behind the bar to give a hand. I never had any bother with anyone in the pub. The Nemo boys were very good to us and the Kerry crowd often dropped by for a drink and a bit of craic.

Life was going well for us around this time – but it wasn't all good.

\* \* \*

Mick McCarthy, who was on the double team, was killed in a car accident in February 1998.

I had a special relationship with Mick. It went back to the time when we were in New York and Leitrim were in the final stages of the

New York championship. Leitrim asked me if I could get anyone to come out and play with the team. I recommended Mick who had played with the Cork minors the year before. He agreed to come and he stayed with me.

The owners of Rosie O'Grady's, Mike Carthy and Austin Delaney, fixed Mick up with a job in construction. He was a really good player and he fitted in very well. He was a great craic and a joy to have around the apartment.

I brought him onto the Cork panel when I became a selector in 1988. Mick went on to captain his club to All-Ireland glory. And he won two senior All-Irelands with Cork.

He was the life and soul of any party. I miss him greatly.

# CHAPTER 26

# *Peace With Meath*

**MY INVOLVEMENT WITH NEMO HAS BEEN A CONSTANT IN MY LIFE AND NATURALLY IT** intensified once I was out of the Cork job.

The first thing I did in 1998 was to organise a good weekend away with the club. I went down to see Páidí in Ventry and we played in his tournament. Páidí had managed Kerry to win the All-Ireland in 1997 and I was delighted for him on a personal level. We had a great time that weekend and it was so enjoyable to sing and drink without anyone looking over our shoulder!

There was a club trip to London later on in the year and we had built up a great spirit. I didn't miss Cork at this stage. Nemo took up a fair bit of time, but I was enjoying mixing with a new group and getting to know a new generation of Nemo players.

Niall Geary joined us from Waterford and Kevin Cahill came in from Meath. They were two fantastic clubmen. They gave me brilliant support. Nemo have been lucky through the years with players coming in from outside. Mickey Niblock, Brother Fabian and Shea Fahy were as Nemo as anyone.

I took the Nemo job every bit as seriously as managing Cork. The preparation and training sessions were planned carefully and I put everything I had back into the club.

We had a good team. Our full-forward line was Colin Corkery, Ivan Aherne and Joe Kavanagh. Niall Geary suffered a bad injury that put him out for the year.

We were beaten by a single point by Duhallow in the county championship after a replay. Seán O'Brien, who was a Cork minor and would later become a Cork senior, was spun around as he was about to shoot the equaliser and, in my opinion, we should have been given a free.

Nemo had now gone five years without winning a county and I said I'd stay on. It was a statistic I was determined to change.

\* \* \*

I was sure 1999 was going to be our year. I made certain we had plenty of challenge games and that kept us on the go.

We drew with UCC in the county final. Colin was carried to the hospital with a heart complaint that could have led to a tragedy similar to Tyrone's Cormac McAnallen. Colin was fine for the replay, but we were beaten by my old club. It was heartbreak for us. We had put in such a massive effort but came up just short on the day.

Donie Donovan died in 1999. We know all about him as a coach. It's down to him that I have All-Ireland medals. When I took over as coach, Donie was always very supportive. He used to go to all the Cork games in Páirc Uí Chaoimh and sometimes my old coach would stand behind the goal and look at things for me. We had a long conversation on the night before we won the All-Ireland final against Mayo in 1999. I took on board everything Donie said. There is no doubt in my mind that he was the best coach I ever had.

\* \* \*

The club's run of bad luck in the county was becoming an obsession. Nemo had done so much for me on and off the pitch. I owed them and once again I put in a huge effort in 2000.

I was a driven man that year and our work paid off – Nemo became the first county champions of the new millennium. We beat Carbery fairly comprehensively in the final. It was our first title in seven years. Alan Cronin was man of the match for us that day. He covered every blade of grass.There had been so many near-misses and now, at last, we were back on top.

\* \* \*

The pub game is a tough life and Mary and myself decided to get out. The long hours were very hard on Mary as she was running the place. We moved out after the Jazz Festival weekend in October 2000.

Naturally, we missed aspects of running the bar, especially the sociable side of it. We had a good GAA crowd coming in, but we were also supported by the rugby lads. Donal Lenihan and Mossy Finn became good friends.

Roy Keane called in occasionally.

We had a chat one day and got on fairly well. Roy is a quiet fella and was always very polite. Roy is a Corkman through and through.

I got in touch with Niall Quinn in 2007 before the All-Ireland final and he set it up with Roy that we could go over to Sunderland to train for a weekend. In the end, the players felt that it would draw too much media attention and we didn't go.

\* \* \*

We were beaten by Crossmolina of Mayo in the All-Ireland club final in Croke Park. Ciarán McDonald was outstanding that day and even though we played well, there was a point in it in the end and we were on the wrong side of it. I've always felt that we left that one after us in the first half but, fair play to Crossmolina, they held their nerve.

That Nemo team showed what they were made of by coming back to win three rounds of the county. James Masters came through that year. I kind of nursed him along until he was ready for the senior team. Dinny Allen had trained Nemo to win the county minor in 1999 and we got a lot of fellas out of that side. David Niblock, my nephew William Morgan, James Masters and Brian O'Regan all came through from that team. The introduction of so many new players didn't come about by accident.

Nemo start off with street leagues when the kids are five or six. We still have all the old Nemo area but there aren't as many kids living there now. A good few of us moved out to the suburbs and Douglas, for example, became a big Nemo stronghold.

There's method and an underlying philosophy that has defined the underage training in the club. Nemo try to give all the kids a game and bring them along. We're not too worried about winning underage titles. Sometimes you have to take off your best players to give the other young lads a game. The young fella who is only barely getting his game at 14 can turn into a star at 21. If I had any advice to give to underage coaches it would be to remember they are dealing with kids. Parents heap pressure on coaches for instant results.

Over-training and too much competitive football has taken enjoyment out of the game. Some children are burned out by the time they come to minor. By then they just get fed up with football and there's plenty of other sports and activities out there for them to try.

I think that's the reason we have a stream of players coming through at Nemo. We try to nurture players and make sure they enjoy their football above all else.

For the county quarter-final in 2001, our goalie Don Heaphy was best man at a wedding and my son Brian came on in goal. He went on to play very well. It can't have been easy for him following in my footsteps but he has always been his own man. I was nervous for him during the game but I had every confidence in Brian.

We were due to meet the 'Barrs in the semi-final, but the game was postponed – for the worst of reasons.

* * *

For most of that summer Colman Corrigan was slagging our two-in-a-row 'keeper and 'Barrs man John Kerins when he complained of a pain in his back. Colman told John it was from picking the ball out of the net.

John Kerins was an outstanding goalkeeper and was underrated. His save against Anthony Finnerty in the 1999 All-Ireland probably won the game for us. Kerinsy, as we called him, had the best and smartest kick-outs I've ever seen. He used to look up as he placed the ball, spot someone 60 yards away and ping him with only two steps back. John was a leader in team meetings and a great character.

Kerinsy wasn't that fond of the physical side of training and he'd always tell you when he felt he had enough done.

When we were going for our second All-Ireland, I got this brainwave that Kerinsy should train for a morning with Phil

Harrington, the Cork City goalkeeper. Phil was well known for his dedication and hard work. Kerinsy was a Garda and there were times when he had to miss training due to work commitments. I approached the manager Noel O'Mahony, who is a good pal, and asked if Kerinsy could train with Phil at a City session.

I dropped Kerinsy to the City training grounds near Cork airport and collected him a couple of hours later. Kerinsy and Phil were still training when I got there.

Phil had a ball about 20 yards away and Kerinsy had to dive on it. This was repeated over and over again. The rain never stopped and Kerinsy was covered from head to toe in mud.

The Garda in him spotted me straight away. He left Phil and the training and walked over in my direction like he was going to arrest me.

When he was at my side of the pitch, he pointed his finger in my direction.

'Don't you ever, ever, bring me down here again.'

I burst my ass laughing. That's the way it was between us. We were more like two friends than manager and player. We grew even closer when he retired and we socialised together. He was always in our group going to matches and was great company.

Kerinsy finally got his back checked out and I got a phone call from Corrigan, his best pal.

'Bill, very bad news. Kerinsy has cancer. We're not sure how serious it is but it doesn't look great.'

John went to see his old Meath adversary Dr Gerry McEntee. The same Gerry McEntee I had the hassle with in the All-Ireland final against Meath. Gerry told John that he hadn't much time left. I broke down crying when I heard the news. McEntee, by the way, couldn't have done more for John.

Colman brought me to see Kerinsy in The Silver Key and we had a cup of coffee. He was practical out.

Kerinsy told me what Gerry had told him.

'I have everything set up, my insurances the lot. Paul and John (his sons) are after getting a place in Críost Rí and I'm as a happy as I could be. I have about six months left Bill and all I want to do is to be with Anne and the kids and drink a few pints every now and then.'

I didn't know what to say. He went downhill fast.

I called to see him regularly. I drove John, Colman and our partners to the 2001 Munster final. The plan was to have a big day out, but Kerinsy took ill and he had to go home early. He passed away just a few weeks later. He didn't even get the six months.

There was a guard of honour at the Lough Church and there was a huge crowd at the funeral. The Cork and Barr's jersey were draped over his coffin.

We all went down to the Lough Tavern afterwards. All the Meath team came along. We had a great night together. That was the night we became friends with Meath. The only pity was that it took John's death to bring us together and we have been very close since then.

We went to the 'Barrs club the next day and we had a day Kerinsy would have enjoyed himself.

The Nemo game against the Barrs game took place a few days later. It was a strange atmosphere. We won by a few points and went on to beat Bantry Blues in the final.

I was walking down to Páirc Uí Chaoimh for the 2009 Munster final between Kerry and Cork when I spotted his son John who is getting more and more like his Dad looks-wise. We had a good chat. It made my day to meet him.

Young John is only 16, and already he is a sub on the 'Barrs minors. John is also on the Críost Rí team. And where does he play? In goal, of course.

His dad was only 39 when he died.

# CHAPTER 27

# *Third Time Lucky*

**NEMO'S GREAT RUN SHOWED NO SIGN OF STOPPING. ONCE AGAIN WE REACHED THE** All-Ireland club final which was played on St Patrick's Day 2002 in Thurles. Our opponents were Ballinderry, the Ulster champions and we were beaten by seven points. They got a couple of goals and that won it for them. We had now lost two All-Ireland Club finals in a row.

I told the lads in the dressing room that it was a game we could have won. 'Nemo lost two in a row,' I told them, 'but so did Cork and then we went on to win the next two All-Irelands.' And I promised the Nemo team there in the dressing room that we would be back in the final again next year.

I had total faith. I wasn't just saying it to cheer the boys up. I meant every word. Before those battles, though, we had to start all over again in Cork later that spring.

Things again went well for us and Colin Corkery got one of the best goals I have ever seen against the 'Barrs in the 2002 Cork semi-final. He got the ball about 50 yards out on the touchline and went past a couple of players. Then from 21 yards out he hammered a shot high into the roof of the net. Absolute class and typical Colin. It wasn't his only moment of magic that year.

We then beat Bishopstown in the Cork county final. Colin, who had been piling up huge totals in nearly every game we played, scored 11 points.

Alan played that day, Brian was sub goalie and my brother Noel's son William came on to win his third county. I was their coach and I never had any bother with the boys.

We played Kilmurry-Ibrickane of Clare in the Munster Club. Alan was corner-forward and William was in the other corner. The two boys played very well and were continually swapping corners. Alan scored a goal and a point, but was sent off deep into injury time and I thought the sending off was harsh.

We won though and then beat Errigal Ciaran of Tyrone in the semi. Peter Canavan was their star and I had Niall Geary play him from the side or behind. And I told Niall to keep him on the outside as much as he could. Niall did a great job on one of the best forwards we have ever seen.

Mickey Harte was their coach and we didn't really get to meet. He is, of course, a football genius and he just stood quietly on the sideline. He didn't interfere with me in any way. I've met him since and I have the height of respect for him.

My prediction came true and we were back in our third All-Ireland Club final in a row against Crossmolina of Mayo who beat us two years previously. We knew Crossmolina would be well-organised as they were managed by John Maughan. We started brilliantly, but then disaster struck. Two of our backs collided accidentally. Niall Geary had to go off. Paul Brophy, son of my boyhood pal Eddie, came on to play his first championship game with Nemo at full-back and he did brilliantly. Martin Cronin, our centre-back, was injured and that was another inter-county player who had to go off. We brought on another young player Brian O'Regan, who is now on the Cork panel, and he did really well.

Gary Murphy went on Ciaran McDonald and had a great game on him. It was tit for tat coming into the last few minutes. We got a free from very far out. One of our players went down injured and I took the opportunity to have a word with Colin. 'If you think it's a bit too far out for you, try to work it in closer.'

Maurice McCarthy came short for the free and he gave it back to Colin who belted the ball over the bar from about 50 metres out on the touchline. It was the best point I have ever seen. In fact, it was the best score I have ever seen in any sport.

Joe Kavanagh kicked another point and we were All-Ireland champions. Alan Cronin scored four points and his performance matched anything I ever saw from any player. I coached him from Under-13 to Under-16 and even then he was heading for the very top.

Alan had no luck with recurring back and hamstring injuries after that final. I think he would have been as good as we have ever seen but for the succession of injuries. William played corner-forward and he had a great game. Brian was sub goalie. Alan was back in the squad. The family are very close. William is like a brother to the boys and it meant so much to us as a family that the three lads won All-Ireland medals.

It also was a vindication of my own belief that we would win the All-Ireland if we stuck at it.

\* \* \*

That summer Cork were knocked out of the All-Ireland qualifiers by Roscommon and Larry Tompkins stepped down as manager.

There was plenty of speculation that I might take over, but I had no approach from the Cork County Board. I had no desire to come back. It was a part of my life that was over and done with. There were several football people in Cork who wanted me to take over, but I had my mind made up. I wasn't going back and that was that.

Then I had an approach from the players. They asked me if I was interested in training the team. I felt I couldn't refuse them. The fact that I was asked to take over by the players swung it. I don't want to sound heroic or anything, but I felt I couldn't let them down.

Frank Murphy called me to ask if I was interested and I told him I was, but I wasn't prepared to go through any interview process. 'Ye know me Frank,' I said. I think he got my drift.

The Board informed me I was the new Cork manager. By then, the rule in Cork was that I could pick my own selectors, bar one from the county champions. I was also free to choose my own backroom staff. I would not have taken the job otherwise.

I picked my own selectors. Colman Corrigan came in from Macroom. Seán Murphy came back again from Kilmurray. Ger Sullivan, a long-time friend, was my man in the stand. Jimmy Nolan came from Castlehaven was the county champions' selector. Teddy Owens was another selector and also our physical trainer.

The selectors had a meeting with some of the Board officers. Frank Murphy wasn't at the meeting. Jim Forbes was the chairman of the

Cork County Board and he was one on the executive who shafted me in 1991.

We outlined our needs for the year. The officers basically said they would have to check with Frank whenever we made a proposal.

Then at the end of the meeting I put out my hand to Jim Forbes and said, 'Let's bury the hatchet. We're both here for Cork.'

We shook on it.

# CHAPTER 28

# *The Second Coming*

**WE MET THE CORK PLAYERS EARLY IN 2004 AND IT WAS A STRANGE MEETING. I HAD NEVER** met such a quiet bunch in my life. They were like mice. And they were totally lacking in confidence.

I always encouraged the players to speak their minds at meetings. Better out than in was always my motto. And I always went into the meetings with an open mind. For me, it was all about taking on board what the players had to say. You had to have enough confidence in yourself to accept criticism from players.

Cork football was never so low. Limerick beat Cork by ten points and the team had been knocked out of the first round of the qualifiers by Roscommon. I was under no illusions to the size of the job I had taken on, but I still had an unshakable belief and I knew if the players worked hard we would be in a position to challenge for an All-Ireland-eventually.

I initially agreed to take on the job for two years. My intention was to build a team to hand over to someone else. When the two years were up, my hope was that Cork football would be back on an even keel.

I went straight to work. We went away for a weekend to the University of Limerick for fitness testing. Teddy Owens took charge of all the physical stuff and I took the football training sessions. . When I came back from New York, I was up to date with the latest training methods but I could see that training methods had evolved and team were much fitter.

I brought in Teddy who was a very good physical trainer and I concentrated on the football side of things. Teddy was a Physical Education teacher and had done an excellent job with the hurlers when they won the All-Ireland in 1999. We played a good few practice games and trained frequently in January and February.

We met Kerry in the league and I felt Padraig Griffin's sending off was harsh in that game. Gary Murphy was reported for an incident with Paul Galvin after the final whistle and was subsequently suspended. Kerry won by two points, but Cork showed a bit of fight that day.

We were looking for new talent, but at the same time we felt the players who played under Larry should be given another chance. Cork drew with Dublin in the league. We should have won it. The ref gave what I thought was a questionable free against us right at the end and it eventually cost us a place in the play-offs.

We needed the games and it was a bad blow. I didn't have much time to get used to the players and they to me.

Our league campaign went reasonably well though and we felt were improving with every game.

I had no dealings with the County Board as a liaison officer had been appointed. And that suited me just fine.

The only persons to remain in the dressing rooms before matches were the players and those directly involved with the team. That meant the County Board officers had to leave the dressing rooms 45 minutes before each game.

I asked the liaison officer to get the County Board out of the changing rooms before the Kerry game and it seemed to work well enough.

The Board didn't have to be told to go anymore after that; they went of their own accord. They had no business in there anyway. I didn't want the dressing room all cluttered up and I wanted the players to have plenty of space to warm up.

There wasn't time enough that year to make major changes. We brought in a few new players. Ciaran O'Sullivan lost his place on the panel under Larry and he and

Colin Corkery came back around then. You could always depend on Colin to get the scores and Ciaran was still very fast.

Cork played Kerry in the Munster championship on the 13th of June. We went down reasonably confident, but we were well beaten. Next up was Clare in the qualifiers. We had to fight hard to get out of Ennis with a win. I thought at the time this might be a turning point, but Fermanagh knocked us out in the next round. We went three points in front into the second half, but Fermanagh hit nine points without reply and they finished up beating us by six.

This Cork team needed a total overhaul. They didn't have the belief they could win. I also felt we weren't fit enough. This was no slur on Teddy who did as much as he could in a short space of time. I felt there was also a lack of hunger and heart. The players were too nice.

I was still involved with Nemo and I coached the Nemo intermediate football team to win the county. I was as proud of that one as any of my wins for Nemo. Brian was in goal and William also played.

At Teddy's suggestion, we went to see our friend Brian Mullins in the UCD School of Fitness. Teddy felt UCD were at the cutting edge of sports science. Brian was now head of sport in UCD and we asked him if he could put a fitness programme in place for us. Brian told us what was involved and it included constant monitoring of the players with frequent trips to Cork by his team to take training sessions.

Such expertise did not come cheap. Brian told us the total cost was thirty grand.

I thought to myself how are we going to sell this to a County Board, who only a few years previously refused me a relatively small sum for a weight training coach.

We were well prepared for the meeting with the County Board. I thought we were finished though when Frank Murphy voiced his objections to our plan, but we made a case and Frank listened. We won him over at that meeting and he came on side. We then had to get the plan past the executive of the County Board. Frank asked all the right questions at our meeting with the executive and but for his help we would never have steered the plan through.

Some players didn't make the new panel, and a few failed to show up for our first team meeting. I let it be known I would not call any player a second time who missed training and as far as I was concerned they were finished with Cork.

Lisa Regan headed up the UCD programme. She had been the weights coach for the Canadian Olympic team for two Olympiads and she was a world leader in fitness management. Her right-hand man, John Barry, was from Wicklow and he was excellent. John had a great way about him and he was very popular with the players. Lisa and John started a fitness programme in September 2004.

The northern teams brought the science of sport to new levels and Kerry followed their lead. We were well behind and I knew it would take time, effort and money to catch up. Still I knew we were on the right road.

There was another worry and that was when I was told John Corcoran was coming in as a selector as the representative of Carbery, who had won the county. He replaced Jimmy Nolan. I need not have worried. He knew his stuff and fitted in very well.

* * *

We decided to go to La Manga in Spain for a week's intensive training in January of 2005. This was no holiday and it was very tough on the players. We did a fitness session every morning. Lisa Regan, John Barry and Teddy took those training sessions. The concentration was on running.

We lunched together and there was rest followed by a football session from 2pm to 3.30pm. I took the football sessions. There was another rest period and then dinner. Lisa took a weights session after dinner and then there was more rest.

The whole trip was very well organised. George Tracey, our sports psychologist, came along with us to La Manga. We were as professional as was possible for amateur players.

The players were brilliant. There was no question of any drinking. The trips to the Canaries were holidays and this was training. That was the difference.

When I came back to inter-county management, I couldn't believe the improved fitness levels. You wouldn't survive if you didn't keep up, or pass out the opposition. Basle from Switzerland trained in La Manga on the same week, as did Wolfsburg and Hamburg of Germany. Our whole set up couldn't have been better organised or more professional – even in comparison to the professional soccer teams. Fintan Goold was another fine young player who came into the squad that January. His remark to Teddy Owens after a training session summed it all up for me. 'Hey Teddy, this is no Saipan.'

Kevin McMahon, John Hayes, Michael Shields, Conor McCarthy, Cian O'Riordan and James Masters were all young players who were now getting their games. And we beat Kerry in our first league game.

Colin Corkery didn't go to La Manga and he dropped out. He was a big loss, but we did very well against Tyrone in the next game even though we were beaten. Kevin O'Sullivan was another youngster we brought in for that game and he played very well. It was all about building for the future.

I celebrated my 60th birthday on the 2nd of February, 2005. My son Brian and his lovely girlfriend Aisling got engaged on the same day. We had a family dinner that night. I felt no different than when I was 59. I didn't feel 60. I was never fitter and still went for my runs. In fact, I planned to do another marathon for my 60th.

There was another weekend in UL when we tried to replicate the training done in La Manga. We must have trained or played on well over a hundred times since January. Football had become almost a full-time job. We played Clare in the Munster championship on June 12th in Ennis, where we always found it hard to win. Cork gave championship debuts to six players. This time though we played well and beat Clare by 0-18 to 0-6. This was a huge improvement from our performance at the same venue 12 months earlier.

There were no drinking sessions in the build-up. The players were totally on side and I think even if I had suggested a booze-up, they themselves would have knocked it on the head. Times had changed. It was very tough on the players but the game had more or less gone professional now. In a way it was a pity but we had to keep up with the top teams who were constantly raising the bar.

Cork were beaten by a disputed goal by Kerry in the Munster final. I felt Declan O'Sullivan accidentally tripped Anthony Lynch and it should have been a free out. We did play well against a very good Kerry team and we beat Sligo in the qualifiers by a wide margin.

You could see the confidence building in the Cork team, but we went into the quarter-final against Galway as underdogs. My father was of course a Galway man and I quoted him to the boys.

'Galway,' he said, 'were poor favourites, but good underdogs,'

The game was played in Croke Park. We were four points behind at half-time but we gave a great second-half display and won out in the end. Brendan Jer O' Sullivan, whose father Kevin Jer played with us when we won the All-Ireland in 1973, got a rocket of a goal at the end of a lovely move and that sent us on our way.

\* \* \*

Who should we be drawn against in the All-Ireland semi-final only Kerry and that was the first ever All-Ireland semi between Kerry and Cork. You couldn't get a worse draw.

The notes of my speech to the lads in the last team meeting reveal a lot and here's the section entitled 'Kerry Myths'...

**1. Kerry are a high fielding team.** *Kerry have no high fielders other than Darragh Ó Sé. They rely on carrying the breaks.*
**2. Kerry are a catch-and-kick team.** *Kerry kick the ball less than any other top-class team.*
**3. Kerry are a clean, foul-free team.** *Kerry have a very high foul count, but do most of their fouling away from the scoring area and are cynical when other teams raise the pace of the game.*
**4. Kerry are a tired team.** *Ó Cinnéide, Russell, Darragh Ó Sé, Kirby, Moynihan and Hassett – their appetite cannot be the same. Playing for 10 years. Must be tired.*
**5. Stand up to them and win the individual battles.**

It was that simple. I always told the players they were every bit as good as the Kerry players they were marking and that approach seemed to work fairly well over the years.

Unfortunately for us, the 'tired' Kerry players were all really good in that semi-final but I was right about the high fielding and Kerry beat us to the breaks. Paul Galvin and Liam Hassett won all the hard ball. William Kirby had an absolute blinder. We were seven down at half-time and I felt we might have a chance if we got to grips with these men. We scored the first point and looked as if we would mount a challenge and then we gave away a soft goal. That was that. The Gooch was brilliant all day and it was a chastening defeat.

They blew us away. We just didn't expect them to be as good as they were. Kerry were really up for it. They were a different team in Croke Park and I suppose we underestimated them.

I had Kerry well figured out, but we just couldn't match them. I stand over the cynical allegation though. Kerry did foul strategically in areas where there was no danger of scoring from the frees.

We were naïve going into that game.

Kerry had changed their style of play under Jack O'Connor. I felt after the defeats to Tyrone and Armagh, they moved away from the traditional Kerry attacking style.

My two years were up. I was nominated again as coach and I decided to stay on. There was no way I was giving up on this team now. We had made real progress.

# CHAPTER 29

# *'Controlled Madness'*

**THERE WERE SOME CHANGES IN THE CAMP AHEAD OF THE NEW SEASON. COLMAN AND** Seánie pulled out and were a huge loss but I did replace them with two great Cork football men, Ger Sullivan and Jim Nolan. Seánie and Colman stayed on as our men in the stands.

The County Board came up with another thirty grand for the UCD team. We continued to bring in new blood.

Kevin O'Dwyer retired after giving years of fantastic service, a couple of which were spent on the bench, and there was never a crib out of him. Alan Quirke was our new goalkeeper and the brilliant young CIT player Donnacha O'Connor came in from junior club Ballydesmond – right on the Kerry border. He was a real find. Daniel Goulding was another new addition. He was a star minor and I liked him from the first time I saw him. We beat Kerry to win the McGrath Cup. At least it was silverware, and the training was, if anything, even more intense.

We came up against Kerry in the league. It was a tough game and I felt Kerry targeted Noel O'Leary. I also felt there was a lot of fouling going on. And straight after the match I couldn't contain myself and accused Kerry of 'being cynical'.

The cynical remark caused fierce controversy. I didn't say it to get at Kerry. I just blurted it out but I stand over what I said. As I always said, keep me away from microphones and reporters straight after matches. I could never switch off the adrenalin and mutter meaningless quotes to the press. It wasn't that I had anything against them.

They have a job to do. I suppose I always turned negative publicity into a positive for us by reading it out to the boys. I wasn't suited to that side of management. It took me too long to calm down after a game. There were incidents with journalists I sincerely regret but there were times too when I felt badly wronged.

We played well against Tyrone who were worthy All-Ireland champions and gave them a good game of it. That encouraged me greatly and confirmed my belief that this Cork team would win an All-Ireland. Kevin O'Sullivan came in for a relegation clash against Monaghan and scored 1-4 to keep us in Division One of the league.

We brought forward the trip to La Manga to May, just before the championship. I want to make it clear that the money for La Manga came from the players' holiday fund and not from the County Board. O2 sponsored the holiday fund and Catherine Tiernan, who was the main woman there, looked after us very well. They were very good sponsors for us.

The players never kicked up at the loss of the holiday fund. That's how dedicated they were, and believe me when I say once again that La Manga was no holiday. It was totally training.

Here's our daily schedule for Tuesday, 30th of May:
*9-9.35am – Team Meeting*
*10.15-11.45 – Beach training session*
*Lunch and rest*
*2-3pm – Gym Session*
*3-4pm – Pool session*
*Dinner and rest*
*7-9pm – Football session.*

We were one of the first teams to go to La Manga and several counties went there afterwards. Our first game of the Munster championship was just a week later against Limerick. We were very poor. I think we might not have had sufficient time to recover from La Manga, but Limerick always gave us trouble.

We were two points down at half-time and it took eight points from James Masters to rescue us. He scored some immaculate points that day. We brought on Michael Prout, Donnacha O'Connor, Daniel Goulding and Seán O'Brien. All four subs were young players and they did very well. We were now beginning to develop a squad as opposed to a team.

We brought in Pearse O'Neill against Clare in a challenge less than three weeks before the Munster final against Kerry and he did so well we not only selected him on the panel, but on the team for the Kerry game. I told the boys we were too nice to Kerry. We had to get in their faces like Tyrone did.

By now we had a new team in place. Pearse O'Neill, Daniel Goulding, Alan O'Connor, Donnacha O'Connor, James Masters, Alan Quirke, Ger Spillane and Michael Prout didn't feature in Larry's time. That was eight new players.

We drew with Kerry in Killarney. We blitzed them in the first half and were 0-7 to 0-1 up. There had to be controversy. Anthony Lynch got sent off when he swung an elbow at Kieran Donaghy. Anthony missed but he was still sent off and I had no great crib with that.

The ref sent off Kieran Donaghy after that and I felt he was hard done by. Kerry fought back in the second half and went two points up with only minutes to go. We battled back for the draw, but Anthony Lynch  would be suspended for the replay in Páirc Uí Chaoimh – or would we?

Frank Murphy mentioned to me the following Tuesday at training that he hoped Anthony would be reported for 'striking'. I thought this was a bit strange as Anthony actually missed Donaghy.

Anthony was reported for 'striking'. His hearing was held in Croke Park a few days after the Kerry game. Frank got him off. Frank's case was that Anthony should have been charged with 'attempted striking' as he had actually missed his target.

Oh, but Frank loved those cases. You could see him get really enthusiastic at the thought of defending a player. One of the boys said if he was ever up in court, he would get Frank to be his lawyer. Frank carried the rule book in his brief case. He knew it better than any solicitor. I think he got more joy out of representing players and officials at these disciplinary hearings than any other aspect of his work for Cork. And of course he had a very high success rate.

Anthony should have been suspended. He got off on a technicality. And then we heard that Donaghy was suspended, even though I felt he shouldn't have been sent off in the first place.

Personally, I was delighted Anthony was back. He was a vital part of this team.

We hand-picked our markers for the Kerry forwards. This was a new thing for me. I just felt it was a case of picking the players who could hold Kerry.

It was a scorching hot day for the replay and La Manga really stood to us. We won the game fairly convincingly. Our full-back line completely outplayed Kerry. We were Munster champions and we had come on considerably since I took over.

Graham Canty tore his cruciate and I cannot over-emphasise what a loss he was. Canty was one of those players you just couldn't afford to lose.

I congratulated the players afterwards in the dressing rooms but I did say in relation to Kerry, 'These fellas are not gone away'.

The team were growing in confidence and we took on Donegal in the quarter-final. I warned the players of the danger of a sense of anti-climax after beating Kerry. I tried to keep their feet on the ground but the next game after beating Kerry is always a dangerous game for Cork.

I told the boys not to tense up just because it was Croke Park. Again I went through some of the negative press coverage. We had a new expression – 'controlled madness' – and that's what I was looking for.

We didn't play well in the quarter-final. Donegal were well ahead until another new boy, John Hayes, stuck in a penalty and Ger Spillane came up from centre half-back to score the winning point. Cork were lucky enough to win and unlucky enough to draw Kerry yet again in the All-Ireland semi-final. There was no getting away from them!

\* \* \*

Our preparations were going well until a letter arrived from Croke Park. I was informed I was suspended for one game for two pitch incursions in the Donegal match. I was stunned. I had some recollection of coming on to the pitch to speak to Derek Kavanagh who was full-back. I was trying to get him to pick up a player. I just couldn't get to him so I ran out maybe 10 yards when the ball was up at the other side of the field.

I couldn't even remember the other incident.

The rule is you can accept the suspension or ask for a personal hearing. I asked for a personal hearing.

Mick Farr's wife Nancy died around then and the funeral was on the same day as the hearing in Croke Park. Mick and I were very close. We worked together as selectors for Cork and his son Mark played for the county in my time as coach. I was very fond of Mark and I knew Nancy well. She was a lovely woman and the Farrs were a fine family.

I had to go to Bantry to pick up a premium. I had to make a living too. From there, I hit for Dunmanway and Nancy's funeral. It was a rush all day. I waited for Mick and Mark outside the church before the Mass. I paid my respects and I would have liked to have gone to the Mass, but there wasn't time.

I rushed to Cork airport, but I didn't make the flight to Dublin and I had to pay for another one. By now I wasn't in good form at all. And all over a triviality.

I made it just in time. Mick Dolan, the chairman of the Cork County Board, met me in Croke Park and advised me to keep the cool.

I cut loose at the meeting.

'What am I doing up here? I remember talking to Derek Kavanagh. How else was I supposed to get to him? I can't even remember the other thing. I have to earn a living and here I am. Here are ye and I'm getting no expenses. . .'

I didn't spare them. 'Ye have a man in the stand watching the manager. It would be more in the GAA's line to have a man in the stand watching the off-the-ball stuff.'

Mick interrupted. 'Billy is a bit upset. His close friend's wife was buried today.' I was furious; there was no way I was going to back off on what I said.

The suspension was upheld and I was in the stands for the All-Ireland semi-final against Kerry.

I was told I could watch the match in a box up the back of the Hogan Stand. There was a monitor in the box and it was primarily for 'the eyes in the stand' or in other words the fellas you'd have watching the game for you who had a better overall view of what was going on.

I had two very good judges doing the job for me. Seán Murphy was a former selector and Cork player. Christy Kearney was also a former Cork player and he had won an All-Ireland Club with Castleisland Desmonds of Kerry. He is a great judge of football and a good friend.

I was only banned from the sideline and I was with the players in the build-up to the game. I was given some sort of a walkie-talkie, but I was getting it all mixed up with this 'over' stuff. I pressed the buttons at the wrong time and anyway I'm not the best at these things, so I gave it to Christy who was more used to it and he sent my instructions to the sideline.

We started well enough and we were level coming into half-time. Then Kerry struck with three quick points. We didn't let them get away from us in the second half like they did the year before.

They were five points up and Kevin McMahon was pulled up when I felt he should have been given a free. That would have made it a four-point game, but Kerry went up the field and scored a point to make it a six-point game.

In my opinion, Darragh Ó Sé got away with several illegal tackles on Nicholas Murphy. He jumped straight into his back with his knees on at least one occasion. Nicholas was injured but he played on.

Michael Shields had to go off after a hard challenge. Ger Spillane was held back when he tried to come forward on occasions and at half-time I told Spillane to put his elbow under the next player who held him back.

Noel O'Leary came on for Michael Prout and he was marking Paul Galvin. There was a fair bit of aggro going on. I was up in the little box in the stands watching the two squaring up to each other. The game was nearly over. I couldn't contain myself. I shouted at the monitor, 'Go on Noelie, go on, deck him'.

We were very disappointed to lose, but we felt we had made progress. The previous year we had been beaten off the pitch but now we were able to stay with them. That's what it's all about with Kerry. You hang in until the end and give yourself a chance of outbattling them.

\* \* \*

I was still involved with Nemo's intermediate football team.

Steven O'Brien was manager and Colin Corkery was also a selector. I missed the county semi-final replay with Glanmire as I was running in the New York Marathon. I was 61 at the time and I was raising money for the Irish Guide Dogs.

Nemo were beaten in that replay.

Steven O'Brien's brother Derek came into the dressing room after the game. The lads were very down.

'It's terrible ,' he said. 'And to make matters worse, Billy is after being beaten in the marathon.'

I mightn't have won the New York Marathon, but I did finish it in four hours, 49 minutes. The race was some thrill. I had always wanted to run in it from my time in New York, but at the end I was totally exhausted. The competitive streak never really leaves you and I pushed myself very hard.

# CHAPTER 30

# *End Of The Line*

**I MADE UP MY MIND THAT 2007 WOULD DEFINITELY BE MY LAST YEAR.**

The UCD team were still on board, although Lisa had to go back to Canada for a kidney transplant and she is getting on fine.

Lisa made an enormous contribution and for her it was more than just a job. John Barry was still with us. We had great time for him. He and Teddy Owens brought us right up a level where we were in a position to compete with any team in terms of fitness.

We were putting in a huge effort, but we just couldn't get anywhere to train that early in the year. Clubs were afraid we would cut up their pitches. John Corcoran's club Ballineen came up with their second pitch. We were very grateful to Ballineen. We wouldn't have been able to train but for them. It wasn't possible to play a match there, but Ballineen couldn't have been nicer to us.

The pitch in Ballygarvan was no longer available. We had to go cap in hand to different clubs. The County Board didn't have a proper venue for winter training. It was a disgraceful situation and it was so frustrating that the biggest GAA county in Ireland couldn't provide somewhere for us to train.

There was more controversy after our first league game against Donegal. The referee Syl Doyle sent off Nicholas Murphy and James Masters, who were two of the quietest players on our panel. I disagreed with the red cards and I said to myself, 'Bill, you better get out of here now before you get in trouble.'

I was held up at the door of the dressing rooms in Páirc Uí Rinn, and who should come along only Syl. I passed a derogatory comment.

'I'll report you,' he said. And he did. I got two months. Once again I rejected the two-month suspension and requested a personal hearing.

There was a couple of very frustrating training sessions in Fermoy. We trained on a small piece of ground about 50 metres by 30 metres.

The West Cork lads had to travel up to 90 miles to train on a tiny area. Again, no disrespect to Fermoy. They were doing their best for us. We made the most of it though and we had good enough sessions.

My hearing didn't go well. We fought the case but the two months stood. I appealed that and the case was heard on the afternoon before we were to play Dublin in Parnell Park. Des Cullinane was there from the Board and he made a strong plea on the grounds we were charged under the wrong rule. We lost again.

I went into Parnell Park and I met the team. I told them what had happened and I couldn't go into the dressing room.

One of the Dublin officials told me to slip in the back to the dressing room and no one would notice. I didn't take the chance. It wasn't that I was had any worries about Dublin taking advantage. I'd be more afraid of one our own fellas reporting me!

Instead, I sat in the stand with Christy Kearney.

We trained in Ballineen the week after and under the rules I wasn't allowed to take the training session. I still drove down to Ballineen.

I parked my car and came round towards the dressing rooms as I wanted to talk to the team before they went out training. Who should be standing at the front door of the dressing room only Mick Dolan, chairman of the Cork County Board. I doubled back before Dolan spotted me.

I slipped in the back door of the dressing rooms and had a few words with the team. Mick had left by then. I spent the rest of the suspension running around different pitches while the players were training. Our next league game was against Fermanagh and I stayed in the team hotel under a false name.

We brought in Michael Cussen, a big full-forward, who would give more height inside. I had seen Cussen play intermediate for Glanmire against Nemo and he impressed me. We won well and Cussen played well. We rested him for the next game against Limerick in the league.

Cork were due to the play Limerick in the championship and there was no way was I going to give them a look at my secret weapon. We won again. James Masters was clocking up Colin Corkery totals in nearly every game. We took him off early and one Cork supporter shouted, 'What are ya doin' Bill. I have him backed to be top scorer in the country.' He won his bet.

There was another trip to La Manga and again it benefited us greatly.

On the last evening, Ger Sullivan and myself were looking down over the pitches and I said, 'Ger, this is it. It's my last year. I'm pulling out. Not a word to anyone.'

\* \* \*

And I finally got to play for Glasgow Celtic. Alan Kerins, the Galway hurler and footballer, set up a charity to help people in Africa. Mick Culhane, an associate director with Celtic, and also a Galway man, agreed to help Alan's project. I met Mick at a few Celtic matches over the years and I became friendly with him.

Mick and Alan organised a charity celebrity soccer game between two teams in Celtic Park in May 2007. Hector Ó hEochagáin was captain of our team and Tommy Tiernan was captain of the other team.

John Giles managed us and Ray Houghton was playing as was Gary Gillespie, DJ Carey, Michael Kiernan, John Higgins, Ken Doherty, Trevor Steven and Greg McCartan.

I finally played in Parkhead. And I almost scored. Gary Gillespie put through a perfect pass, but just as I was about to shoot my hamstring went! I still haven't heard the end of it.

Seán Fallon came down to say hello. His daughter was with him and I hadn't seen her since she was a kid. Seán was well into his eighties by then but was as nice as ever. The occasion turned out to be a great day and Alan's African projects in Zambia picked up a nice windfall.

Playing for Celtic was a huge thrill – even if it was 34 years on from that trial. Maybe that's some kind of Celtic record!

\* \* \*

We were scheduled to meet Limerick in the Munster championship. There was the usual warm-up in the gym in Páirc Uí Chaoimh before the Limerick game. The dressing rooms are far too small for 30-plus players, selectors, physios and back-up staff. I made it clear that I only wanted the people who were directly associated with the team in the dressing rooms.

We came down from the gym to our dressing room about five minutes before we were due to go out on the pitch. I was in the middle of my last few words to the lads when the door of the dressing room opened.

It was Frank Murphy. There was barely enough room to open the door. I was in mid-speech.

'Frank, excuse me,' I said politely.

'I'm sorry, Billy,' said Frank just as politely and he went to close the door on the inside.

'Frank,' I said, 'excuse me, would you mind leaving us alone for a minute?' This was said in a very quiet tone.

Frank left the dressing room without a word. And he never spoke to me for the rest of the summer. I knew for sure the expulsion from the dressing room wasn't going to do me any good in terms of my relationship with the Cork County Board.

We met Kerry a couple of weeks later. Michael Cussen came out to midfeld and he curbed Darragh Ó Sé. We fought back from a six-point deficit.

Derek Kavanagh was put through two minutes from time and his jersey was pulled. It was a clear penalty but we didn't get one. The Sunday Game analysts confirmed it was indeed a penalty. Marty Duffy was the ref that day and he didn't see it. The decision annoyed me greatly and that anger would have very serious repercussions for me later in the championship.

Kerry won it with two brilliant long-range points from Kieran Donaghy and Seán O'Sullivan but we felt very hard done by.

We beat Louth and Sligo in the qualifiers. But we lost James Masters with a broken jaw. He was a huge loss but by now, we had a very strong squad.

We had 33 players in the panel for the Sligo game. The GAA rule was we could only tog out 30. I could see the disappointment in the three lads' faces as they stood near the indoor warm-up area. I felt terrible for the boys and I vowed to myself that this is never going to happen again.

We had three injuries for the semi so that meant everyone was togged out.

John Fleming, who owned the Sheraton Hotel on Fota Island, gave us the use of the superb hotel facilities. There was a very good gym and an excellent pool. Training was going well and the players were in top shape for the semi-final against Meath.

I didn't bring up the battles of the late eighties and early nineties. We put all that bitterness behind us when John Kerins died.

We put in our best performance since I took over. We destroyed Meath. The final score was 1-16 to 0-9. We played a running, high-tempo game and we matched them physically.

Kerry beat Dublin in the other semi-final and that set up the first ever All-Ireland final between Kerry and Cork.

John Fleming again gave us the use of the Sheraton Fota for a weekend in the lead-up to the match and we tried to replicate our La Manga experience.

We played the usual A v B game a week before the final. Anthony Lynch broke a bone in his wrist. It was a catastrophe. Dr Con told us he had no chance of playing in the final. Anthony had a fantastic year. He was one of our best and most experienced players. A massive loss.

We held our final team meeting after a pool session in the Sheraton on the Thursday night before the game. I kept on emphasising to the players that all the pressure was on Kerry. I told the boys that 'everything Kerry have achieved over the years would mean nothing if we beat them. Just go out and play. All the pressure is on them'.

I roomed with Frank Cogan on the night before the match. And the following morning as I was putting on my tracksuit, I said, 'Frank, this is the last time I'll be putting on this.' I really had made up my mind to quit.

We had 33 in the squad and as far as I was concerned every player was equal. I received reassurances from the chairman that the players would be togged out numbers 1-33. The Board would possibly get fined for togging out more than the permitted 30 but other counties had done that in the recent past. Remember these men had trained every bit as hard as the 30 on the squad. I felt the Board should take the pain.

It was agreed that we would tog out 33, but on the day of the match the three extra players were handed ordinary Cork jerseys while the rest of the squad were given the official Cork jersey with the All-Ireland final crest on the front. That really upset me. The three over and above should have had the official jerseys. It's the kind of thing you show the grandchildren. Once again I felt terrible for the three left out.

Rules are rules but as far as I was concerned players come first.

\* \* \*

I thought we had made sure the lads wouldn't be nervous by adopting a strategy that put all the pressure on Kerry. In fact, both sides were very tense and the football in the first 20 minutes wasn't great. I didn't think we would be that keyed up. Looking back on it I suppose most of our players were playing in their first All-Ireland. The Gooch scored a punched goal and that was the difference between the teams at half-time.

I was still very confident we would win. Then two minutes into the second half we gave away another goal. One of our defenders was dispossessed by Kieran Donaghy and he stuck the ball into an empty net. Our 'keeper was off his line looking for a pass. It was a bizarre goal.

That totally settled Kerry and a few minutes later Donaghy again stuck the ball into an empty net when two of our players collided.

One of the Kerry players was holding a Cork player off the ball and I brought it to the attention of the linesman Marty Duffy, who was the referee in the Munster final when we were denied a penalty.

I was critical of Marty over that penalty. More fallout.

Kerry won and I'm not saying they didn't deserve to win, but we had no luck. The goals were freakish and I wouldn't blame any of our players. I felt worse for the players than myself. If the game was played again a week later, we would have run them very close.

\* \* \*

I had a policy of never going into the losers' or winners' dressing rooms after matches. I always thought it was hypocritical. You go in to and say, 'Tough luck. Hope ye win next year.' I didn't care whether they won next year or not.

If you're beaten, you go in to the winners' dressing room and say, 'Well done. Ye deserved it', while inside you're really saying in your head 'well get lost, ye shower of...'

This time, though, I felt I should go in to the Kerry dressing room. It was my last game with Cork and I had never been in a Kerry dressing room before. I went down the line to shake hands with the Kerry management after the game. I shook hands with the Kerry manager Pat O'Shea and I met my close friend Dave Geaney, who was a Kerry selector.

'Billy,' he said, 'will you come in?' I knew what he meant.

'I will Dave,' I said.

I walked up to the Kerry dressing room on my own. That was the way I wanted it. I gathered my thoughts on my way up the corridor.

Mick Dolan, the chairman of the Cork County Board, was there before me and he had just finished his speech. I slipped in at the back. There was a hush in the dressing room.

'I just want to say something about all this stuff about hating Kerry. Of course I do,' I said. 'The same as I hate Dublin when I'm playing against them. The same as I hate Limerick or any other county when I'm playing against them. That's just for the match but when it's over, its over and life goes on.

I have more connections with Kerry than any other county. First of all, that fella standing over there – Dave Geaney – was the first man to pick me in goal. He started me off in UCC and looked after me.

I spent one of the happiest years of my life when I was teaching in Kerry and I wouldn't have come home, but for football. Gerald McKenna, the ex-chairman of the County Board, looked after me and I had the good fortune to play with one of the greatest players of all time, Mick O'Connell.

Someone wrote this was a very poor Kerry team. That's not true. There are men in this dressing room who would hold their own in any era with any Kerry team. I think I'm qualified to say that.

Well done. It's ye we aspire to. I just wanted to set the record straight.'

The Kerry players clapped. I think they knew I spoke from the heart.

\* \* \*

Mary and myself went to Spain for a week's holiday. I had a big decision ahead of me. Most of the 2009 Cork panel were with us back in 2007 and I knew they could only get better with age and experience.

Mary felt I should pack it in, but as ever she said, 'Billy, I'll back you 100 per cent if you want to stay with Cork.' I mulled it over and over and over as I walked along the beaches.

I texted my close friend Jim Cremin and let him know I was going to pull out. Jim texted back, 'Don't do anything a while'.

All along I assumed the position was mine to accept or refuse. We reached an All-Ireland final and while things didn't go our way, it was still a massive achievement. I had no reason to believe I was going to be shafted.

Mick Dolan went public after the Meath game and said that as far as he was concerned, the Cork job was mine for life.

There was some criticism that I played James Masters before Daniel Goulding because James was a Nemo man. It was also stated that Daniel was unhappy because he wasn't getting more playing time and that he was thinking of quitting the panel.

Over the years I could have picked Nemo men as my co-selectors, but I always ensured there was a spread from around the county. James had been out with a broken jaw. Seán Boylan sent on a container of herbal medicine and it seemed to speed up the recovery process. James had been top scorer in the country that year and he was going well in training. You couldn't leave out the top scorer in the country.

In my mind I always picked the best players – irrespective of their club. I would never do that to Cork or to any player. Question my ability all you like, but never question my integrity.

Daniel Goulding called me in response to the criticism to say he was totally happy with the way I managed the team. That meant a lot to me. I always had great time for Daniel. There was also an allegation that Eoin Cadogan was thinking about pulling out of the panel because he wasn't getting enough game time. Eoin called me to say he too was perfectly happy with the set-up. Another great young lad.

Around this time I got a letter from Croke Park charging me with using abusive language towards Marty Duffy in the All-Ireland final. I had a choice of either accepting a ban for six months or I could appeal the decision.

I was shocked when I heard I got six months. I appealed.

The night before the hearing Derek Kavanagh phoned me. It was a call that had a profound effect on me. Up to then, I had made up my mind I was going to retire as Cork manager.

'Bill, there's a number of the Cork players who want to accompany you to the hearing to show solidarity'. I told Derek there was no point as they wouldn't be let near the hearing and they could be hanging around outside for ages. I was very moved by the offer and the following day as I travelled up on the train, it got me to thinking that maybe I owed it to as good a bunch as I ever came across, to stay on as manager.I had already decided it was going to be my last year, but the fact the players were prepared to travel to Dublin to back me up meant so much. I wasn't sure whether I was coming or going.

And this time who came up to Croke Park to defend me, only Frank Murphy. This was the first time he had spoken to me since the incident when I asked him to leave the dressing room before the Limerick game in June. We appeared before the appeal committee in Croke Park and Frank was absolutely brilliant.

His knowledge of the rules and his legal arguments were as good as any senior counsel. He made mince meat out of the prosecution.

We were told we would have to wait for the result. I shook Frank's hand outside the room and thanked him for his defence.

'Frank,' I asked, 'if I get the six months, does that rule me out from managing the Cork team.'

'Don't worry, Billy,' he said. 'We'll cross that bridge when we come to it'.

The next day we were notified that the suspension was reduced from six to two months. Then at the next meeting of the County Board, my old adversary Bob Honohan proposed Cork should go back to the system whereby the County Board appointed the manager and selectors. It was carried almost unanimously. I had no notification this was happening.

I am certain that there were many in the County Board who now expected me to resign as I only took the job on the condition I would appoint my own selectors. I decided I wouldn't resign just yet. I'd let them sweat. I called team captain Derek Kavanagh and told him I couldn't accept that system. I was going to resign. Derek wasn't surprised. 'We were afraid of that,' he said.

I went off to New York for the marathon with my nephew Rory, Mary's son. He's a great guy and great craic. We ran in the marathon and I hoped to improve on the previous year. Once again I was beaten. I was ten minutes slower, but I did it in 4 hours, 59 minutes.

When I came home, I decided to write a letter to Frank informing him I was not prepared to work under the proposed system. Later that day, Frank Cogan called in to see me.

'I wasn't going to tell you this,' he said, 'but I had a phone call from a County Board man asking me to tell you to pull out. The Board man said 'I'd hate to see Billy getting hurt and they are going to shaft him'.'

Dinny Allen was on holidays in Spain and he had a phone call from yet another Board man. The Board man told him, 'We don't want to see Billy hurt. Can you get him to pull out before they shaft him?'

I felt they were trying to get at me through my friends. It would have much easier on them if I pulled out.

\* \* \*

The Board appointed good old Teddy Holland as manager and good old Liam Hodnett as one of his selectors. These were the two men who were appointed back in 1991, the last time I was shafted. Teddy Mac, Diarmuid O'Donovan and Mick O'Loughlin were also appointed.

The players issued a statement – they were going to fight this all the way.

Their plan was to get the Board to revert to the old system.

It was at this stage that Conor McCarthy, Graham Canty and Eoin Sexton called to me in my office. Their support was very moving. I had the players on my side. That was all I cared about.

\* \* \*

The footballers went on strike and the hurlers joined them. I didn't have any more to do with the strike after that. It was now coming into the Christmas season and there was still no resolution.

And then I got that heart attack. I was lucky I didn't have to go for a bypass. The doctors put in a stint and that kept the blood flowing. And but for that shower of rain on Kinsale golf course I might not be here today.

I was only just out of hospital when Mary's mother Julia Mai died at the age of 92. She was a wonderful woman and we always got on very well together. Tough times for Mary.

But I still managed the odd laugh in spite of all my troubles.

Dinny Allen, who was as ever one of my staunchest supporters, tells about the day he was at Mass and he noticed Frank Murphy standing in the pew in front of him. It was right in the middle of all the controversy. It came to the part of the Mass where the priest asks everyone to shake hands.

Frank turned around and put his hand out to Dinny not realising who was behind him.

'Peace be with you,' said Frank and the two shook hands.

'And what did you say?' I asked Dinny.

'Peace be with you.'

'What?

'Ah but Bill, I didn't mean a word of it.'

\* \* \*

I still felt really bad. It was just before Christmas and I was affected more psychologically than physically. I kept on thinking, 'How could this have happened to me? I'm so fit and then bang'

It probably took me six months to get over the heart attack and all that went with it.

The players were still on strike. There were massive protest marches and the Cork supporters gave the players huge support. I knew it was only a matter of time before the players would win.

Eventually, the Board agreed to arbitration and guess what? They agreed to let the manager pick his own selectors. I was still recuperating from the heart attack. Conor Counihan was appointed manager and of course he picked his own selectors.

And that was the end of my 40 years with Cork.

The hospital gave me an exercise programme and I followed it to the letter. It started off with five-minute walks and then ten-minute walks. A far cry from the marathon.

Bit by bit, I started to feel stronger. Then I started running.

# CHAPTER 31

# The Passing Game

LOOKING BACK ON IT ALL NOW, I SUPPOSE THE FIRST THING I HAVE TO SAY IS THAT I HAD A good life of it. My journey can be divided into many trips, but each and every one is linked and is part of what I am today.

All GAA careers start with the club, but Nemo is more than just a GAA club. It's a way of life. The values of friendship, sportsmanship, and the drive to succeed are a statement of who we are.

I've been a member of Nemo for over 55 years and consider myself blessed to have become part of the club. Nemo has been accused of being 'clannish'. We probably are. I can't disagree with Frank Cogan's statement that you never see a Nemo man on his own.

I'm glad to say that I can still see this united mentality in the club today.

The young lads all knock around together in big groups just like we did when we were their age. My sons are fierce friends with Dinny Allen's son Conor and Jimmy Kerrigan's son Paul.

It's the same carry-on: slagging, football and hurling, a few beers and looking out for each other. The camaraderie between the lads strengthens my confidence in the future of the club. This was something that developed simply by being part of Nemo. We didn't push it by saying 'go on, be friends with Dinny's young lad' but the structures are there and, by and large, the club is run the right way.

There are still fellas active in the club who were working away when I was underage. Paddy O'Sullivan, Finbarr O'Shea and Derry Kenneally were there from my boyhood days and they are still as involved as ever. There are many more too numerous to mention.

Nemo have grown from a small, homeless junior team to one of the leading clubs in the country. We have a magnificent complex now.

I look back over the years and remember when we were like nomads moving around from one piece of ground to another. There are four outdoor playing fields in the new Nemo. We have an all-weather indoor pitch, an all-weather outdoor facility, numerous club meeting rooms, large state-of-the-art dressing rooms, a gym, a bar and a club shop. We're very proud to have such a magnificent complex, especially considering the club's humble beginnings.

I don't see myself as having contributed any more to the club than the trainers of the young lads, like the Under-12s or Under-14s. There are lots of unsung heroes who played a significant role in the club's success. I trained the senior team most of the time and we have done well.

The fellas who have stuck with the underage teams down through the years don't seek any recognition, but make a huge contribution to Nemo. Maybe I can claim some credit for developing the Nemo style. Nemo play the same brand of football from the underage teams right up to senior. When minors step up to senior, the style of football is nothing knew to them; they have been reared on it.

Nemo has a strong but fair disciplinary code. The kids know what's expected of them and they are not only better players, but it develops them for life.

And there's a great sense of fun in the club.

Brendan 'Hacker' Hurley is another great character who was around back since as far as I can remember. He organised the annual Nemo golf trips to Spain.

Brendan fell into bad health in recent times and his legs had to be amputated.

He might have lost his legs, but he didn't lose his sense of humour.

'I've a new song Bill.'

'What's that Brendan?'

'I'm not half the man I used to be.'

There's an over sixties singing competition in Cork every year. Brendan is a fine singer and someone asked him if he thought he would win it.

Brendan said, 'I'll not only win it but I'll walk away with it.'

'Wrong Brendan,' said another great Nemo man, Dinna Driscoll. 'You won't walk away with it, you'll wheel away with it.'

That's real Nemo.

\* \* \*

Even when I was training Cork, I always remained involved with Nemo at some level. I did what I could for the club. I saw it as a payback for what Nemo did for me. The club gave me something to belong to. We didn't have any extended family in Cork and Nemo filled that void for me. And of course I loved playing hurling and football.

It could have been the teacher in me, but I always wanted to improve the players I coached, both as players and individuals. It could be that was the reason I got so close to the players I trained.

I'm now involved with the intermediate footballers and junior hurlers. I've always loved hurling. Back in the fifties, Nemo was more of a hurling club than a football club. We won the intermediate county hurling championship and brought the team up to senior level. The senior team did well for a couple of years although they were a small bit unlucky not to make the county final. Unfortunately, we have slipped back down to junior level.

I would hate to see hurling dying in the club. I was only too glad to accept the position of junior hurling selector because the club was trying hard to keep hurling alive. The junior county is very hard to win, but we need to get back up to intermediate. John Coogan is training the junior hurling team and he has put an awful lot into it. I'd love to see us winning the junior county and I will do all I can to get the club back up.

Maybe that sums us up. We stick together and we don't give up.

I have to say that I have mixed feelings about leaving the Cork job. You can't just wipe away 40 years. I don't miss the pressure or the County Board and it's lovely to be able to go to the games as a civilian. You can enjoy a drink before the match and you don't feel you are carrying the expectations of a whole county on your back. I miss working with the lads. I have great time for this current bunch of players.

Things were up in a heap the first year I came back, but the final three years that followed were as happy as I ever spent with any team. They were more than willing to learn. These young lads gave the training programmes 100 per cent. Disciplinary issues never arose – no one ever had to talk to them about drinking. This Cork team were just a dream to work with. And I so felt for them when they went down to Kerry in the 2009 All-Ireland final.

Yes, the players make big sacrifices. But I don't think Ireland could sustain the professional football and hurling. Even if we wanted to go professional, I don't think we could. Professional GAA would ruin the club scene. The players would become the property of the county team. I would hate to see that happening. I do not agree with the players looking for pay, but I don't see that happening either.

I think they should be given more generous expenses. There are lots of demands on inter-county players, who lose out financially because of their commitments to the game. At the highest level, hurling and football is professional in everything but name, especially considering the time that's put in. And I agree with the formation and recognition of the Gaelic Players' Association. I do not believe their ultimate aim is pay for play. The GPA was born out of the way we players were treated over the years. What you sow, you reap.

Our 2007 final defeat by Kerry was devastating. I had pity for the team because if any bunch of players ever deserved to win an All-Ireland, it was this crowd.

I have always enjoyed my time with different Cork teams over the years. There was the 1966-'67 team who helped a rookie goalie establish his place for Cork. We had great characters in that team.

Of course the '73 All-Ireland winning team will always hold a special place in my heart. We got on very well back then and we still remain the firmest of friends. We didn't manage to win much after that but it was back in the days of a great Kerry team and there was no back door.

The 1987-1991 team were the most successful in Cork football but even if they never won a match they were a great bunch to work with, and we never lost sight of the fact that football can be fun.

We built a new team over the next six years. That squad was unlucky not to win an All-Ireland and again, I wouldn't swap one day I spent with them.

My ambition was always to play with Cork, but I thought that if I ever made a Cork senior team, it would be the hurling team. When I finally made it, I had fierce pride, and still have, in the Cork jersey. Many helped me on the way. Donie Donovan of course and Donie Wallace of Cork Hibs taught me so much about goalkeeping.

And I'd never look for pay for training Cork. It doesn't interest me. When Dan Hoare was Cork treasurer, he asked me to tot up my expenses, I asked him what expenses and he said for driving down to training. I said it's only a couple of miles. He gave me a nominal sum at the end of every year to cover travelling and phone calls.

As for my detractors in the County Board, most of them have never pulled a Cork jersey over their heads. It's only criticism if you accept it, and I refuse to accept it from them. The people who really mattered supported me and their back-up kept me going.

When I took over Cork in 2004, it wasn't for any glory or ego, it was to develop a team. Twenty-three of the players we brought in were on the panel for the 2009 All-Ireland final against Kerry. Cork lost that one but we are not far away from winning Sam. Have faith boys.

I was in The Sunnybank Hotel the morning after that match and I had three surprise visitors. Darragh Ó Sé and his brother Tomás came out from the city to see me. I was so honoured. I always liked the two boys even if we had our battles on the pitch and I knew them since they were kids.

'We have someone, a young lad, who wants to meet you. He's outside the door. Is it okay if he comes in?' asked Darragh. It seems 'the young lad' wanted to check first if I would see him. Paul Galvin came in the door.

'Billy', he said,' I just came to wish you well.' Paul has been in more scrapes than myself and we had a few run ins during the course of Cork- Kerry games. I was just amazed he was there on the morning after he won the All-Ireland.

Darragh and Tomás were waylaid and I found myself on my own with Paul. He was very shy and his head was down. I could see some of myself in him.

'Billy he said,' I always wanted to meet you. I showed the video of you on the sideline to my pupils and I told them that was the kind of passion you needed in football and in life.' I made a new friend that morning.

In a way, I'm just lucky to be still around.

Prior to the heart attack, my diet was reasonably good, I exercised regularly. I was just after running a marathon. So I was shocked, as was the doctor, who said that I wasn't a likely candidate for a heart attack.

The medics confirmed the stress of those terrible days in 2007 might well have caused my heart attack. The doctors said it might also have been hereditary. My father died of a heart attack. The doctors told me I might not have survived if I hadn't been so fit.

Since then, I have stuck fairly rigidly to my fitness programme and have watched my diet. I'm lucky in the sense that I don't have a sweet tooth, but I still have a few pints in The Idle Hour with my friends every Friday evening. That's good for the heart.

If there was a match on a Saturday or Sunday, I'd have a few drinks afterwards but that's it. I'm not a big spender.

With regard to my business, the bad times have hit me, as they have hit you all. As everyone knows, times are particularly tough in the financial game at the moment. You just have to keep battling away. But I have the belief that things will come good. They always do. After every crash, there's a rise.

Yes, I have had a good life and I am proud of my achievements but I'm not perfect by any means. I'd say my temper is my Achilles heel. I wish I was cooler.

I have reacted with my fists at times. I think that when my mother died there was a certain anger left in me, even though I was young at the time and didn't really have the chance of getting to know her. And then when Tony left, I felt I lost someone I loved and looked up to. I feel terrible after I lose the head but there are times when I just cant help it.

The rest of my family are calmer. My father was a very cool, placid man. Noel is the same. My sister Mary is well able to control her emotions.

Some fellas would be delighted when I'd react to bullies or whatever. I just can't walk away when I see wrong-doing. Injustice really gets to me but that's no excuse for losing the head and the fisticuffs.

Despite the fact that I lost my mother when I was five, I think I've been lucky in my family life.

My father was rock-solid. He didn't praise me too often, but behind it all I think he was quite proud of me. I think that was the way the fathers were in those days. There wasn't much by way of outward displays of love, but you kind of always knew it was there and would manifest itself at certain times like when you were in trouble, or on the day you won your first All-Ireland.

I'm crying now as I think back on it and now that I'm older, I know he really did care for me. I think back to 1973 when I captained Cork to win the All-Ireland. I look at the old days in pictures. That's just the way I think. It's like a photo album. My father is there before me wearing his good overcoat and my sister Mary looks so good in her up for the match finery.

My father and Mary had trouble getting into the Skylon Hotel for the post-match reception, but they made sure they got to see me. My father didn't say much, but you could see he was delighted. I'd love to have him here with me now to thank him for all he did for us.

Then there was Noel, who didn't go to my matches in the last few years. He was so nervous for me. He's like my Dad, rock-solid, and he's a fella I look up to very much.

My sister Mary gave me great support always. She cooked for us and took me on as someone she was going to look after no matter what. I used to be accused of being spoiled because I was the youngest but I don't think I was. I had to make my own way. We all had to.

There was only just my Dad, Tony, Noel and Mary when I was a boy but now we have a large extended family. My sister Mary's kids, my wife Mary's nephews and nieces and Noel's family and my daughter-in-law Aisling are all very close. There's no excuse to be lonely now.

I was blessed to meet my wife Mary. She came from a similar background to myself. Her parents were country people and her Dad was steeped in the GAA. We often talk about the values we share – things we did at Christmas, Sunday dinners, love of family and, of course, the GAA .

Mary loves the GAA and never flinched when I was going through tough times. We have two good lads for sons. I'm very proud of Brian and Alan. They are better men than me. That's all you can hope for.

Alan said to Mary only the other day, 'I'm glad Dad isn't involved in the big matches anymore because now I can watch the match without my stomach churning'. I understand how he feels because my stomach is churning for them now when they play for Nemo.

Yes, they are Nemo boys too. And Corkmen.

And so it goes on to the next generation. That's what it's all about.

The passing game.

# FACT FILE

## As a player

**With Nemo Rangers:** Seven county medals, four Munster club medals and two All-Ireland club medals

**With Cork:** One All-Ireland medal, five Munster championship medals and one National League

**Also:** two Sigerson Cup medals, four Railway Cup medals, one All Star and one Texaco footballer of the year award

## As a coach

**With Nemo Rangers:** 11 county titles, 10 Munster club championships and four All-Ireland clubs

**With Cork:** Two All-Irelands, eight Munster championships and two National Leagues

**Also:** One Manager Of The Year award

# APPENDIX